PLAYING with FIRE
Creative Conflict Resolution for Young Adults

FIONA MACBETH & NIC FINE

Published in cooperation with The Leaveners/Leap Confronting Conflict and the National Youth Agency

NEW SOCIETY PUBLISHERS
Philadelphia, PA   Gabriola Island, BC

Inquiries regarding requests to reprint all or part of *Playing with Fire: Creative Conflict Resolution for Young Adults* should be addressed to New Society Publishers, 4527 Springfield Avenue, Philadelphia, PA, 19143.

ISBN Hardcover	USA 0-86571-305-7	CAN 1-55092-256-4
ISBN Paperback	USA 0-86571-306-5	CAN 1-55092-257-2

This book was originally published in the United Kingdom in 1992 by Youth Works Press, 17-23 Albion St., Leicester LE1 6GD in conjunction with The Leaveners (Quaker Arts Project), Leaveners Arts Base, 8 Lennox Rd., Finsbury Park, London N4 3NW.

Cover design by Judy Lamarind of Parallel Design, Inc. Original interior illustrations by Gary Hitcham. Printed on partially-recycled paper using soy-based ink by Capital City Press of Montpelier, Vermont.

To order directly from the publisher, add $3.00 to the price for the first copy, and add 75¢ for each additional copy. Send check or money order to:

In the United States:	*In Canada:*
New Society Publishers	New Society Publishers
4527 Springfield Avenue	PO Box 189
Philadelphia, PA 19143	Gabriola Island, BC V0R 1X0

New Society Publishers is a project of the New Society Educational Foundation, a nonprofit, tax-exempt, public foundation in the United States, and of the Catalyst Education Society, a nonprofit society in Canada. Opinions expressed in this book do not necessarily represent positions of the New Society Educational Foundation, nor the Catalyst Education Society.

Contents

Preface

THIS course is aimed primarily at professional trainers in the youth service – that is, at those responsible for running training programmes for youth work professionals and volunteers. But it is intended for use with all those who work with young people – not only in youth clubs but in residential homes, special needs centres, youth training programmes, the penal service, volunteer projects, and further and higher education. And it will be found useful by workers who are running training within their own staff team. It is envisaged that the training will ultimately be passed on to young people themselves. Materials specially adapted for use with young people, including a selection of exercises from this manual, can be found in the companion publication *Fireworks* (Youth Work Press, 1992).

The exercises in the course evolved in various ways. Some we developed through our own working experiences; others we adapted from ideas and materials that we came into contact with along the way. We have explored many ideas which were originally conceived by others, and we appreciatively acknowledge their contributions to the materials in the course. We would like to give particular credit to the following people and organisations, whose inspirational work has greatly helped us in ours:

- Alternatives to Violence Project (AVP), New York City, USA
- John Bergman, Geese Theatre Company, New Hampshire, USA (in particular, ideas for Exercises 14.5 and 17.3)
- The Breakthrough Foundation, Youth at Risk Programme, San Francisco, USA (in particular, ideas for Exercises 17.4 and 17.5)
- Richard Cohen, School Mediation Associates, Massachusetts, USA (in particular, for ideas on role-play and mediation)
- Conflict Resolution Network, New South Wales, Australia (in particular, ideas for Exercise 14.7)
- Geese Theatre Company, Birmingham, England
- Advisory, Conciliation, and Arbitration Service for their contribution to ideas in Exercise 18.8
- Centre for Intergroup Studies for ideas from the *Directory of Nonviolent Action* contributing to Exercise 23.4
- Gil Fell and Mary Synott for Exercise 4.1
- Albert Nolan, of the Catholic Institute for International Relations, for ideas contributing to Handout 23.3
- Southwark Mediation Centre for ideas contributing to Handout 20.5

We are indebted to Alec Davison, and to the Leaveners and LEAP committees and staff, for encouragement, support and unfailing enthusiasm for the work; likewise to all those who have contributed as participants on LEAP training courses and projects. Thanks also to Pippa Marriott, who undertook the initial editing of these materials, and to Omaid Hiwaizi, who originally word-processed them.

Note on usage   In order to avoid sexist language, we refer throughout these materials to 'he' or 'she' as 'they'. Though grammatically incorrect, we felt this to be the best solution to the difficulties raised by the absence of a generic singular personal pronoun in the language. We hope that readers will appreciate this concern and forgive the resulting grammatical inaccuracies.

INTRODUCTION

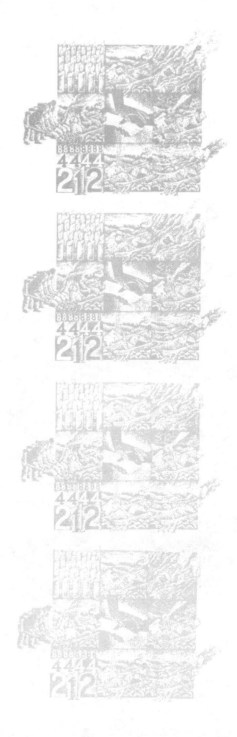

Conflict: danger and opportunity

THE characters that make up the word 'conflict' in Chinese are *danger* and *opportunity*. This course has been produced to offer those working with young people the chance to discover and develop ways of finding the opportunity as well as the danger in the conflicts within their personal and working lives. The course works on the understanding that there is potential for growth and positive change in any conflict.

Conflict is not necessarily destructive – in fact it is a vital part of life and growth. Much growth involves pain. Conflict becomes damaging when it is ignored or repressed, or when the only responses to it are to bully, bulldoze or withdraw. Destructive conflict frequently means resourcelessness. This course aims to enable participants to build up their own personal skills and supportive structures so that in their responses to conflict and violence they can draw upon a whole range of rehearsed and established resources.

The course offers a structure within which participants explore situations of conflict and potential violence, primarily in the workplace, practise skills for dealing with them, and rehearse possible strategies and techniques for future use.

Values and assumptions

THE key principle embodied in this course is one of *individual respect*, the trust that every human life is valuable. We need to be able to respect ourselves; we need to respect others. We all want and deserve to be heard and to be fairly treated. This is the message of the course and therefore underlies its conduct and process. Tolerance, non-judgmental attitudes and acceptance need to be experienced from the first session onwards and established as its practical ethos. As trust and openness develop between participants, changes and shifts in attitude become possible. Few of us can grow under threat or in fear.

All participants need to feel that they are valued and respected, even when admitting to behaviour that others in the group may find unacceptable. To be shouted down is not only to lose face but to suffer an act of personal violence. This course chooses to make a stand on a disposition towards non-violence. Behind it lies a recognition of the fact that unfairness, injustice and lack of basic resources tend to provoke violence, which in turn tends to escalate into more violence. Oppression, tyranny and imperialism may seem to leave no alternative but violence in the face of suffering, brutality and conquest. But violence will always leave legacies of hurt, of bitterness, of vengefulness and destruction, and has brought bloodshed and death which will never be forgiven. Violence diminishes the violent as well as the victim. This course argues that in our personal conflicts violence and disempowerment can be avoided if alternative behaviour has been rehearsed and prepared for.

The ethos of mutual respect will foster a shared understanding of *democratic processes*. Communication and co-operation lie at the heart of the democratic way, and at the heart of the course's approach. The group provides a practice-ground for much of what the course teaches. Through the patterns of feedback and reflection, the group will come to feel that it owns the work, its directions and its style; and regular consultation and sensitive response will allow participants genuine freedom to make well-informed choices. Democratic participation is both rewarding *and* challenging for the individual. The democratic style of groupwork therefore involves creating a supportive environment in which learning can take place through working together, having space to be heard, listening in depth to each other when genuine inter-group conflicts arise, not putting each other down, seeing the issue from the other's point of view, making contracts or new agreements and regularly checking these out to see if they are working.

The philosophy and values of the course are underpinned by a belief in the essential *creative potential within each individual*. We are born with an urge to play and create, to be curious and inventive, to experiment and to explore: it stays with us from cradle to grave. Our upbringing and education either affirm and legitimate that urge or they smother it, repressing it with inhibitions, denials, rejections and discouragements. Under these repressive influences, our energies can be deflected into apathy, cynicism and all manner of alternative addictions from shopping and materialism to drugs and violence. Yet those very symptoms are indications that our creative energy is not extinguished but bent out of true. With caring support, good encouragement and new opportunity, creativity can be nurtured through the cracks in the concrete, and can flourish into more positive human relations and enhanced personal well-being. The course trusts that change and growth will come as our creativity is released, and that such release is possible, in some degree, for every one of us. Confronting conflict is about tough love. It is about keeping on believing that change is possible.

The learning process

THE theory of the course is to be teased out of its practice. There is no formal didactic input. Each session needs to be properly introduced, but it is from the experience of the exercises and reflection upon them that understanding will come. This is no longer a new method. Most current developmental learning materials follow the fourfold process of EXPERIENCE, REFLECTION, NEW UNDERSTANDING, and NEW EXPERIENCE (as 'changed' participant).

The course materials are rich in opportunities for *experience*. It is the facilitator's responsibility to provide equally generous opportunities for *reflection*. Time needs to be allowed at the end of each exercise, session, and section of the work for participants to discover the general lessons to be learned from the input and the particular implications for themselves. Some time for feedback and discussion is built into the course, but this is the absolute minimum. Ideally the 60-hour module needs an additional 20 hours for reflection and assimilation. A one-day-a-week experience of the course offers ample opportunity for this between sessions. Course learning can be further consolidated if the facilitators are able to follow up participants and help to support new practice and experiment in 'real' situations.

Good reflection needs sensitive facilitation which acknowledges feelings and personal history yet holds the experience together for the whole group, keeping things moving and keeping to some agreed agenda and time structure. It is important to sustain the energy and direction of the work. Strategies for achieving this are developed further in the section entitled *TRAINING FOR TRAINERS*.

During the course the particular needs of some participants will become evident. Such work revives buried feelings and forgotten hurts that have never been fully assimilated. The facilitators will need to be prepared to give good pastoral care to the group and allow opportunities and structures for participants to care for each other. It is helpful to have two facilitators, so that while one is leading the session the other can be available to support a participant in need.

Before the course begins, local counsellors and voluntary support services need to be researched so that any immediate need is responded to quickly and without fuss. It will be helpful if the facilitators themselves are trained or experienced

The structure of the course

in pastoral care to help in reading and responding to signs of distress. Appropriate responses may be befriending, hugging, listening privately, or perhaps professional specialist help. It is also vital to establish links with agencies for drug, sex abuse or mental health counselling. Essentially the facilitators need to be open, warm, non-judgmental, accepting and positive, pedlars of no political party or religious line, and careful trustees of the group's growing vulnerability and openness.

The use of drama and role-play

Much of this personal sharing, risk and openness is encouraged in the course by the use of drama, role-play and simulations. These techniques enable the participants to rehearse the skills and strategies that are developing. Practical rehearsal of this kind is the only way to move from 'head' knowledge to 'whole-self' knowledge, where the feelings and emotions, the body and non-verbal communication can be engaged simultaneously with our thinking and reasoning. It is a holistic approach that does not put down the rational and analytic but argues that this must always be in partnership with an education of the feelings, which, in the end, are the provocation for most destructive and violent conflict.

Drama operates at normal life speed, whereas a lecture condenses and selects. Drama puts us at risk, draws from our unique well of life experience, engages the feminine and masculine dimensions in us all, brings the intuitive and spontaneous left-hand part of our brain into play alongside our linguistic and rational right-hand mode of being. We think and feel on our feet just as we would in reality. The physical enactment of a difficult situation can be a more accurate way of assessing both the problem and its possible solutions. On reflection, we can examine our behaviour and our interactive style and be helped by others, and by our own insights, to try new and alternative responses.

Through their experience of the interactive group techniques of the course, we hope that any mix of participants will gradually form a group. Some of the work is specifically geared towards achieving an atmosphere of group trust and cohesion, the importance of which cannot be overstressed.

THE manual is in ten sections, of which eight form the 60-hour training course. The *INTRODUCTION* and *TRAINING FOR TRAINERS* are not included in the 60 hours but are vital reading for the trainers. **They must be read first**.

Each of the eight sections of the course focuses on a different aspect of conflict and identifies particular skills and techniques for confronting and dealing with it. The first six are practical, each deepening the work and each named according to the stages a fire goes through before erupting into a blaze. This analogy with fire is used throughout as a clear and direct means of representing the causes and escalations of conflict, one which will be immediately understood by young people. The seventh section, *MEDIATION*, concentrates solely on mediation as a tool for resolving conflicts. It assumes that the skills and techniques of the first six sections have been learned. The eighth section, *SOCIAL CHANGE*, looks at the positive potential of the fire analogy, with the blaze representing social change.

Conflict and fire

From the beginning of the experimental work that led to the evolution of this course, there was a concern to encourage young people to see the work of confronting conflict as something daring, exciting and challenging. It takes great courage to be a mediator. There is nothing insipid about being a peacemaker in a war game, whether within a family or a youth club or between nations. Conflicts release overwhelming personal energies and it is a brave person who has the guts to step in when the situation is ablaze. Young people found the fire-fighter a more robust image than the peacemaker, and the work soon took off using the fire analogy as a simple way of enabling young people to see how conflict escalates. The analogy can facilitate a memorably quick analysis of the stages of conflict; and it can help us to see conflict, like fire, as a good servant and a bad master.

As the work explored the concept of fire, the course developed into an extended 'fire drill' of skills and strategies for coping with everyday and professional situations of conflict. Like fire, conflict has the energy and power to heat and to hurt. Conflict and fire grow in much the same way. They are both dangerous. When harnessed, however, fire can provide warmth and energy; when confronted, conflict can facilitate both personal and social change. Just as fires have incendiaries, fanners and stokers, so conflicts have the embittered, provokers and agitators. For positive transformation they clearly need listeners, persisters and mediators. Positive transformation is always possible. This whole course is underpinned by the understanding that there is both a destructive and a creative potential in fire and in conflict.

A schematic application of the analogy, in both its negative and its positive dimensions, is provided on page 7.

Social change and empowerment

The key impulse behind these materials is to encourage those working with young people, and through them young people themselves, to confront the problems that surround them and to do so with appropriate resources and support. Through the course, with its ample practical opportunities for self-development, it is hoped that the confrontation of conflict can be made an empowering and positive act rather than an act of violence.

The course is designed to encourage participants to build up their resources, skills and understanding from a position of self-respect, for when we begin to respect ourselves we begin to respect others. We hope that these materials will encourage participants to see confronting conflict as a way of living up to their huge potential to create rather than destroy.

How to run the course

THE course is divided into eight seven-and-a-half-hour sections, each of which contains three two-and-a-half-hour sessions. Each of the eight sections can be used independently, as can each of the sessions, and ultimately each of the exercises. However, these materials are primarily intended to be used as an integrated training course. It is not a book of exercises to be dipped into to suit any occasion. Some materials more suited to that way of working are listed in *TRAINING FOR TRAINERS* (pages 26–27). Each section builds on work covered earlier, as does each of the sessions, and all are designed for in-depth rather than one-off use.

The course could be experienced over twelve working days of six hours (two two-and-a-half-hour sessions plus one hour for reflection). These could be weekly over a 12-week period (which has the virtue of allowing plenty of time for assimilation) or brought together to make an intensive two-week course. A course of 24 two-and-a-half or three-hour sessions, daytime or evening, with additional follow-up, is another possibility. Finally, four or five weekends scattered over a year would be a good but probably expensive possibility.

TRAINING FOR TRAINERS covers essential ground for running any of the course work – even one session. All the work is focused on personal growth as well as skills and resources training, and many of the exercises will encourage participants to draw on their own experiences. Many people find this work probing and demanding on personal resources. Looking at our own anger and facing the anger of others is not comfortable. The work needs to be guided with confidence, understanding and skill in order to establish and maintain a secure environment in which challenge and change are possible. The course is therefore intended for use by trainers who are skilled and experienced in leading group work and facing the challenges and rewards of fluctuating group dynamics.

FIRE, CONFLICT AND CHANGE

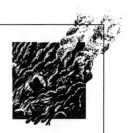

Conflict

PEOPLE
Whenever people are in contact with each other, there is potential for conflict. This potential will vary according to the different degrees of combustibility in the individuals.

INCIDENT
There are always tensions and disagreements between people. Some of them can cause a spark which ignites conflict.

BROODING
Tensions and grievances are smouldering away but are unexpressed. The conflict feeds off rumour and gossip.

AGGRAVATION
Those who are interested in agitating the situation provoke it further. Feelings of anger and hurt may be expressed as prejudice and hate.

ESCALATION
The situation is intensified by the outside pressures of the social environment. Prejudice and disaffection add to the conflict.

CONSEQUENCES
There is a blazing conflict in which some people are damaged. No-one involved is untouched by it.

Fire

THE FUEL
The raw material of the fire. Some of it is highly combustible. Some of it is damp and flame-resistant.

THE SPARK
Friction causes sparks to fly. Some land on dry wood and it catches alight.

SMOULDERING
The fuel catches alight and begins to smoke. There is an indication of fire.

FANNING THE FLAMES
The wind blows and the smouldering fuel flickers with life. The flames lick and leap.

STOKING THE FIRE
The fire consumes the fuel. It demands more. Huge logs are piled onto the fire.

THE BLAZE
The fire rages. It is a huge blaze. It will not die down easily.

Change

PEOPLE
Whenever people are in contact with each other, there is potential for challenge and growth. Different values, opinions or aims contain raw issues and fuel for fire.

FLASH OF INSIGHT
There are always raw issues in a community or relationship. Sometimes a flash of new insight can bring an issue alive for an individual.

TENTATIVE RESPONSE
The individual looks for shared concern from others, making an initial response to the issue.

ENCOURAGED ACTION
Those showing concern for the issue grow in number, encouraging and supporting each other.

INCREASED RESPONSE
Response to the issue increases. The possibilities of achievement inspire action from many.

EFFECTIVE ACTION
Aims are achieved. People celebrate the blazing fire. It is a beacon which lights, warms and inspires.

TRAINING FOR TRAINERS

Using the manual

IN this manual, the course follows a built-in 60-hour schedule. The overall structure and balance is known to work, but different facilitators will no doubt want to alter or adapt parts, leave some out and extend others. Each facilitator should trust their own discretion and knowledge of group dynamics and processes. In a recent 60-hour course the two trainers used only a quarter of the material, focusing on a few exercises from each section. This was in response to a request from the course participants to work in a way which allowed plenty of time for exploration and development of each exercise.

The sessions

In all there are 24 two-and-a-half-hour sessions. At the beginning of each session, time is allowed for a brief introduction, whose aim should be to provide a clear focus for the session. For continuity, this could include a reminder of the focus of the previous session's work.

Each section (which consists of three sessions) opens with its own contents list and a general introduction, including a summary of its focus and aims, and lists of key concepts and key questions.

Reflection

The final ten minutes of each training session are allocated to reflection.

Participants should be encouraged to share their views and feelings on all the work they have done and whether the experience has been useful to them. During the reflection it is a good idea to remind the group of the original intention of the session. They can then evaluate the success of the session by referring to its intended aims.

The introduction and reflection are important components of each session. They are opportunities for the facilitator to show respect for the participants, by making sure that they know what they are doing and by listening to and taking into account their views.

The exercises

Each session has 130 minutes' worth of practical work, made up of exercises of different lengths. Some sessions include as many as eight exercises and others just one or two longer ones.

A time allocation is given at the head of each exercise. For guidance only, this suggests the minimum time for the exercise to be properly explored. If further time is needed on a specific exercise, facilitators can create it by removing another exercise from the session at their own discretion.

The text of each exercise is presented under the following headings:

Description Indicates the central focus of the exercise and whether it is carried out individually, in pairs, small groups, or in one large group, or a combination of these.

Aims Summarises the key learning areas for the exercise.

Directions These are numbered to indicate the order in which the instructions should be given, with the time allowed for each stage.

Feedback and discussion Suggests questions that the facilitator might ask to encourage discussion and reflection among the participants. The nature of the questioning is at the facilitator's discretion, using our suggestions as a guide.

Notes Suggestions, tips and comments for the facilitator. Sometimes we suggest ways in which the exercise could be extended.

Skills Lists the key skills that are needed as well as those that are developed in the exercise. The course assumes a certain level of literacy among participants – familiarity with the written word, and reading and writing to the standard of the average school-leaver. However, there are ways in which the work can be adapted for those with reading or writing difficulties. Pairing up members with different strengths and weaknesses to support each other can often be productive. On the other hand, some of these exercises can be incorporated into literacy work with the specific aim of strengthening skills in this area.

The participants

The exercises gradually become more and more demanding. They ask more of the participants, and they require trust within the group and a safe environment to work in. The early exercises concentrate on group dynamics and communication in the hope of establishing an atmosphere of trust and group cohesion. In certain circumstances confidentiality will have to be established.

Ideally, the trainer would want more time than the two-and-a-half hours indicated for a session. It would be good to include some 'light and livelies' to relax the group and create an atmosphere of fun and togetherness, at the start of the session as well as between some intense and difficult exercises. We would suggest the use of icebreakers and trust exercises when any group meets for the first time. It is also a good idea to have a relaxed wind-down at the end of each session. Some ideas for warm-up and wind-down, including group-reflection exercises, are suggested later in this section (pages 20–26). The resource list (pages 26–27) suggests books that you can refer to for further ideas. We recommend that you have at least three hours available for a two-and-a-half-hour session. (This would, of course, extend the duration of the course from 60 to 72 hours.)

In some sessions facilitators are given a choice of exercises. This is indicated under the contents list at the beginning of the session.

Single-sex work

Two of the course exercises involve single-sex work. Such work could be incorporated elsewhere at the facilitator's discretion. Single-sex work can give participants the freedom to explore issues and feelings that they might find difficult to deal with in the presence of the opposite sex.

It is often illuminating for groups to separate to do similar work, and then to regroup at the end of the session to share their experiences.

Single-sex work should be seen and experienced as a positive working method rather than a divisive one.

Running sessions

The physical environment

THE physical environment in which sessions take place is important. Consideration should be given to noise levels from adjoining spaces. If the session deals with sensitive matters, it is best to have a private space that is not used by others for access and where it is possible to work uninterrupted. If the session is going to be particularly active, then the size of the space is important. If the exercises in the session require that the group subdivides, alternative small spaces may need to be organised beforehand.

Think about lighting and heating. There needs to be enough light for participants to feel that they are working in a bright, welcoming place. Natural light is always best. If you are reliant on artificial lighting, it is worth checking what kind of lighting it is. Working under fluorescent lights with a low ceiling for long stretches can cause headaches. Fresh air in the summer months is always welcomed, as is sufficient heating in the winter.

It is good to have at least one wall on which large sheets of paper, wall-charts and visual aids can be displayed. This area needs to be well lit. A flipchart which can easily be removed is a great asset.

Establish whether the working space is going to be used for smoking, drinking and eating, during working hours or in breaks. It is always better to have an alternative space for participants to relax in between sessions. This means that there is a clear distinction between 'work' and 'non-work' space.

Have clear guidelines for maintaining and respecting the space in which the group works. These should take in such matters as smoking, eating and casual chat. The less clutter, disturbance and distraction, the better the chances of focusing the group. A clean floor is important if any practical work is being done or if participants are going to sit on the floor rather than in chairs. Floor mats, cushions or rugs will be useful.

Starting on time is important for group morale. Getting a commitment from participants to attend regularly is also important to the trust and stability of the group and therefore vital to this kind of work.

Facilitating group work

Setting definite time limits on the exercises, discussions and reflections provides a strong framework and promotes discipline within the group. It can also help maintain a good pace and flow during the session. If more time is needed this can be negotiated and extended, rather than running over time with no clarity or sense of purpose. The facilitator should aim to put enough pressure on the participants to achieve specific tasks within a definite time limit. Often the shortest time limits produce the most exciting work. However, facilitators need not feel that running over their intended time limit on an exercise is a failure. There is little value in keeping time just for the sake of it.

Every exercise has a feedback and discussion period at the end of it, and every session ends with time for reflection. It is important that these periods are well structured and well facilitated. The more the group becomes used to disciplined and brief comments, the less the facilitator will be required to order the proceedings. All participants should be aware of the time limits and of the method being used in feedback or discussion. Methods are suggested both later in this section and within the exercises. Some of these are particularly useful for getting the group to talk openly while tensions are high. Group dynamics need to be constantly monitored, and grievances should not be allowed to become stored or buried. The course includes mediation and negotiation exercises which can be useful in getting problems into the open.

Clear instructions and guidelines for all the exercises are essential. It is also a good idea for the group to establish its own working methods and practices, and there are a couple of exercises in the course which encourage this.

A team of two facilitators is always a good idea. There are several advantages to this: mutual support, continuity, balance (male/female, white/black, or whatever), different styles and strengths, sharing preparation and facilitation tasks, the possibility of working simultaneously with two small groups, demonstrating a model of teamwork and co-operation.

Facilitators could encourage participants to lead certain exercises in the course by giving them the text of the exercise in advance – the day or weekend before – to allow preparation.

Apart from its benefits for those doing it, leadership from within the group can give facilitators a break and revivify the group's interest. Participants could also be encouraged to adapt the exercises to their specific working environment.

Group numbers for this kind of work could be between 8 and 16. Intimacy is important. A group of 12 working with two facilitators is ideal.

A circle is an effective structure for general group work. The sightlines are good and it provides a feeling of equality and security for the group.

Trainers working with people with disabilities may have to adapt some of the exercises and games according to the needs of the participants in their group.

Equipment and resources

The exercises require minimal preparation of material resources. Some will require the photocopying of handouts or the preparation of stimulus cards. Essential resources are a flipchart (or large sheets of paper and a supply of Blu-tack), marker pens, scrap paper, and pens. Any items necessary for suggested games (blindfold, beanbags, or whatever) are readily available.

Structuring courses

The 60-hour course

THE 60-hour module can be presented in many different ways. The most intensive would be working an eight-hour day over ten days. A typical day could be:

10.00	Warm-up	*15 min.*
10.15	**Session 1**	*90 min.*
11.45	Tea/coffee	*15 min.*
12.00	**Session 2**	*90 min.*
1.30	Lunch break	*60 min.*
2.30	**Session 3**	*90 min.*
4.00	Tea/coffee	*15 min.*
4.15	**Session 4**	*90 min.*
5.45	Wind-down	*15 min.*

This schedule is extremely tight. It does not allow for any flexibility, unless some exercises are left out to create extra space for others. What we have found valuable, especially at the end of an intensive training day, is to have an open hour during which the participants decide what they would like to do. They might choose to explore a theme not included in the programme, to develop a specific exercise further, or just quietly to consolidate the day through discussion. The final session could itself be left open. This would provide time which is less intense than the rest of the day and where the agenda and process are determined by the participants rather than the facilitator. For people who are not used to this kind of work, the days can prove quite exhausting – for facilitators as well as participants.

Weekend courses beginning on Friday evening and ending late on Sunday afternoon can also be structured around a selection of the material. (For example, a weekend could focus on communication and assertiveness, or personal and social change.) It is possible to get in about fifteen hours of work over a weekend. The whole course could be presented over four weekends.

The course could be presented over a 24-week period (one night a week) or over a 12-week period (two nights a week).

Style of courses

Residential courses are a good idea. Away from their normal environments, participants can focus on the work without being distracted by everyday responsibilities. Residentials also have the advantage of allowing participants to interact throughout the weekend, in the periods between and after sessions. This informal interaction can be invaluable in developing group cohesion.

The sole advantage of the one-or-two-evenings-a-week or one-day-a-week model is that participants have more time to absorb the material and reflect on the work. They might even have the opportunity to try out some of the practical work in their own working environment. The main disadvantages of such staggered training are that it takes time to get the group going after a week's break and that people are likely to be tired at the end of a working day.

There is a strong case to be made for organising training courses and sessions whereby youth workers and young people (staff and clients of a youth centre, for example) are trained together. There are many ways in which they can learn from each other. Such training changes the usual power dynamic, providing an ideal opportunity for workers and young people to build mutual trust and understanding. (This would, however, involve making adaptations to some exercises.)

Planning and evaluation

It is important that participants are properly informed about the course before it happens. The information they receive should be clear, accessible and precise, so that they know exactly what to expect and what is expected of them. Holding an advance meeting, during which questions can be answered, is useful and will help to iron out any misunderstandings.

Planning should be as thorough as possible. The aim is always to have your energies and concentration fully on the work once it commences.

Evaluation, follow-up and support are important components of any training process. Evaluation of the course could take various forms. Participants could be asked to fill in formal evaluation sheets at certain points in the process. A large sheet of paper permanently on the wall could be used as a 'graffiti' board for informal comments and moans. Or participants could be asked to fill in a report a couple of weeks after the training, having had the opportunity to reflect on it. They could be followed up a month or two later to see if they are using the training in any practical way. The facilitators could even offer work visits to the participants, and further training specifically designed to meet the participants' needs.

Course focus

The structure of the manual follows the development of a conflict, using fire as an analogy, and the exercises are grouped accordingly. However, it is possible to regroup and reorder the exercises for a different focus. For example, in a recent *Confronting Conflict* course the trainers took intervention strategies as the focus, highlighting the four areas of work outlined below.

Internal intervention   Intervening in our own thoughts and emotions – that is, what goes on inside us – with the aim of taking more control of our reactions and responses to difficult situations and potential conflicts.

Personal intervention   Intervening within an interaction with another person or group with the aim of being assertive about personal needs and perceptions.

Second-party intervention   Intervening between another person and what is going on for them internally (for example, when they are expressing bigotry or hatred), with the aim of exploring their underlying emotions and needs (for example, looking at their own 'enemy' within themselves).

Third-party intervention   Intervening as a third party between individuals or groups involved in a dispute, with the aim of enabling the disputants to come to a mutually acceptable resolution.

A breakdown of the training exercises under these four headings is included as Appendix 2 (page 174).

Techniques and methods

Role-play

AN active process whereby participants explore issues by enacting specific roles. This technique is used to rehearse strategies for responding to certain situations, and to enhance participants' confidence in applying those strategies. Role-play is fully explained on pages 17–20.

Hot-seating

Otherwise known as *in-role questioning*. A technique whereby participants question or cross-examine a character in role to find out more about a specific situation – for example, what motivated the character to do what they did. This is also a useful way of developing a character for a role-play. In finding answers to the various questions put to them, the participant develops a clearer idea of their character – age, family, neighbourhood, opinions and so on.

Brainstorm

An efficient technique for getting ideas from a group without lengthy discussion or questioning. Setting a strict time limit for the exercise (probably just a few minutes), the facilitator asks a question such as: 'What are your immediate responses to the word "teacher"?' The participants call out their very first thoughts. Single-word replies or short phrases are best. A scribe writes the responses on a large sheet of paper visible to the group.

All contributions are accepted without question. Nobody offers any criticism or comment at this stage. If a contribution is made in the form of a long sentence, the scribe attempts to shorten it to one word or a short phrase, with the approval of the contributor.

Through brainstorming you can get an immediate impression of the range of responses in the group, and glean material for further development. You can go on to group related words under various themes or headings. This works well when introducing a new area of exploration.

The brainstorm is a lively tool which encourages group participation. It is not threatening, as only short contributions are asked for and no judgments are made.

Tableau work

A quick and active way of establishing the thoughts and feelings of group members without having to verbalise. Tableaux (otherwise known as *photographs*, *frozen images*, or *statues*) can be created individually, in pairs, in small groups, or in a large group. A tableau might be created in response to a word – anger, for example. The participants would form their body into a shape that they felt corresponded to the theme. They might hold their fists up as if wanting to strike out at somebody. They might, on the other hand, present a more abstract physical image of angry thoughts and emotions. The facilitator might suggest that the participants form themselves into groups according to their interpretations of anger. All the aggressive images could combine to make a group tableau. All the withdrawing images could also form a group tableau. If you combined the tableaux together you would have a large tableau or photographic image to represent the entire group's response to the theme.

A development of this work is to ask all the frozen images to vocalise one thought each, or one word each. Participants could also move in slow motion from one frozen image to another – for example, from one interpretation of anger to another. Participants could sculpt each other, or one participant could sculpt a whole group tableau around a specified theme or situation. (*Sculpting* involves one person moving another, or others, into a gesture or position by physically placing them in it – for example, raising their hand in the air – or explaining verbally what they want them to do, or indeed demonstrating what they want. The person being sculpted holds the position as if they were a statue.

Tableau work is an excellent way of expressing and exploring thoughts and feelings physically rather than verbally. Tableaux can be used to explore a wide range of themes or issues – family, community, school, employment, relationships, aggression, unity, division, and so forth.

Improvisation

When we improvise we respond intuitively to specific situations, making things up on the spot and making do with what we have at our disposal. As a training activity, improvisation is an extension of role-play. The participants might know who they are and what situation they are in. But they will still have to improvise, as they won't know what will be said to them or how they will respond. This activity can build confidence in everyday situations in which you have to respond quickly and think on your feet.

Feedback

This can occur at any stage of a session – before an exercise is to begin, during an exercise, or after an exercise or group of exercises. The purpose of feedback for the facilitator is:

* to check that the learning aims for the session or the specific exercise have been achieved and that the group is ready to proceed
* to check that the group dynamics are supporting the work and that tensions are not causing any blocks in the process
* to check that individual group members are coping with the process

The purpose of feedback for the participant is:

* to ask questions and seek clarification when they are unsure of anything
* to comment on any problems they are experiencing
* to give support to fellow participants
* to give the facilitator any suggestions as to how the process could be improved
* to acknowledge how they are feeling about the work

Reflection

This normally occurs at the end of a session, a day or a course. It is an opportunity for participants and facilitators to assess and take stock, to reflect quietly on how they are responding to the work and to the process as a whole. It is an essential part of the learning process.

Reflection can occur in silence, or in discussion prompted by questions from the facilitator – perhaps a combination of both. It could end with a brief group sharing. It is often useful to go round the circle asking each participant for one word that expresses how they are feeling, or a sentence encapsulating the key thing they have learnt, or something

Using role-play

bad and something good about the session, or perhaps one thing they had wanted to say during the work but hadn't. Group discussion techniques such as the whip round and the bracelet (see page 25) are useful for reflection. The value of reflection is explained in more detail in the *INTRODUCTION* (page 4).

Warm-up

At the start of a session this gets everybody ready for the work ahead, both mentally and physically. The warm-up aims to create a relaxed group feeling and an atmosphere of trust, and re-establishes a focus for concentration within the group. It is a chance to forget about your journey in or a conversation at lunchtime and to build an energised and purposeful environment.

Wind-down

At the end of a session this prepares the group for departure by getting rid of any tensions or worries arising from the work, and aims to leave them with a positive, relaxed feeling. This aim will have been partly achieved through reflection, but a short period of silence or a quiet activity exercise that unites the group can be an affirmative way of ending a session.

R OLE-PLAY is one of the tools used in the training course to offer a particular kind of learning experience. We use role-play primarily to teach skills, and to offer the practical experience of using those skills. For example, two participants might role-play disputants so that other participants can practise skills in listening and mediating.

It is important to make a distinction between the different types of role-play with their different purposes and focuses.

Dramatic characterisation

Main characteristics Focus of role-play is on individuals. Participants take on characters very different from their own, building and exploring various personae. Improvisation is story- or character-based.
Learning area Discovery of someone else's point of view, seeing the world through another's eyes. Personal challenge in finding ways to express ideas and emotions as another person.
Emphasis Play and fun, the dramatic development of a character and a story, and the creation of theatre.

Personal discovery and therapeutic role-play

Main characteristics Focus is on an individual, and a learning area for that individual. The other role-players are there to support this focus. It offers the opportunity for an individual to face fears, and to practise coping with personal difficulties.
Learning area Personal discovery in a chosen area of difficulty for the individual.
Emphasis Personal growth for an individual in the group. This type of role-play is used in many therapeutic settings. For example, a male inmate might role-play his return to society, with other role-players providing the obstacles and barriers he will come up against. This inmate is faced with the likely reality of his release, and his reactions to obstacles. The role-players support his discovery.

Task- and skill-oriented role-play

Main characteristics Focus is on the group task. Each individual has a role which contributes to the whole; but the task is for the group, not for the individual. The role-players have a function to fulfil, not merely a character to play.

Learning area Particular skills such as mediation or assertiveness.

Emphasis The aim and the learning area of the particular role-play. When planning this type of role-play take care that role-players are not asked to assume characters very different from their own (do not ask a 22-year-old to play an old woman). The role-players' focus needs to be the group task, and not whether they are realistically playing their character.

These three areas are not isolated from each other. There will be personal discovery in all of them, and through developing a character we may discover and use new skills. But it is important that the focus of the role-play is clearly within one of these areas. Each serves different kinds of aims, and each demands different kinds of instructions for the role-player – for a task- or skill-oriented role-play they need to know what their functions are, rather than (say) their age.

Much of the reluctance surrounding role-play is generated by the fear that acting is expected. This is true of dramatic characterisation, where the role-player's task involves working on the truth of a *character*; but it is not true of task- or skill-oriented role play, which involves playing a *role* – an aspect, not the whole, of a character. It is helpful to maintain clear boundaries between these two disciplines.

In what follows we concentrate on the use of task- or skill-oriented role-play.

Planning and setting up a role-play

Key questions to ask yourself as facilitator

Why role-play? Why are you planning to use this particular tool? What do you think is the value of it in this instance?

Why this particular role-play? What is the aim of this role-play? What do you hope to achieve with it? What is its purpose?

What will be required of the role-players? What will be needed from them, collectively and individually? What kind of roles will they be playing?

What is the previous role-play experience of each participant? How much introduction and warm-up will be needed? What skills can you rely on? What kind of explanations will be necessary?

Checklist for planning a role-play

Schedule Allow time for your briefing, for the role-players to prepare (if necessary), for the role-play to run, and for debriefing and evaluation.

Numbers How many participants? What size groups will you divide them into?

Information What do you need to say? How will you say it? This includes the principles of role-play (do you need to explain the difference between 'being a character' and 'playing a role'? do you need to draw distinctions between the different kinds of role-play outlined earlier?), as well as the focus of this role-play (what is the aim of this role-play?) and defining individual tasks (what information is essential, and what is unnecessary? what is the key task for each player to hold on to?).

Facilitation Who will be facilitating each group? What methods will they use? What techniques should role-players be prepared for? (Some relevant techniques are covered on pages 19–20.)

Debriefing Who will do the debriefing? What method will they use? (See page 20.)

Evaluation Who will run evaluation? What are the key questions? What time will you allow?

Introduction and briefing

Your role-play is now planned. You are ready to brief the group. Prepare a checklist for yourself of the information you need to give. For example:

- general (role-play principles)
- specific (aims/focus of this role-play)
- individual (individual tasks)
- practicalities (time, numbers, and so forth)

Be ready to answer questions and queries from role-players before they start preparation.

It is always useful to have the in-role characters wearing a name-tag: this will help the players to take on characters other than their own, and other participants will not have any difficulty remembering the characters' names.

Tips for role-players

- Be clear about your role, and about your responsibility within the role-play.
- Be open to, and aware of, the roles and responsibilities of others within the group during the role-play.
- Check that you are clear about the purpose of the whole role-play.

Key questions for observers

- What messages or communications are being transmitted, either verbally or through body language?
- What options are being explored for resolving the conflict?
- How are the characters listening to each other? What quality of listening is apparent?
- What can you tell about the power relationships between the role-play characters?

If there are several observers, each can take a different area to observe. If not, one observer can decide which areas to concentrate on.

Role-play in action

Boundaries and rules

How will a participant stop the action if they feel they are losing control and unable to continue? What methods will you use to stop the role-play if, say, the action is getting nowhere? How should players show physical violence – should they 'freeze' before the action? Participants should be made to feel that they can stop the action if they feel uncomfortable or threatened in any way.

Intervention techniques

Stopping and processing   Role-players come out of role. The facilitator questions the players about what is going on. For example: What are your aims? Are you accomplishing them? If not, what is stopping you? This method is useful when the role-play is not working well, when it seems that the players have lost direction. By asking them questions you are not giving them your answers. The role-play is still in their hands. Encourage them to find their own answers to the difficulties they are facing.

Hot seating   The facilitator stops the role-play. The role-players remain in role while the facilitator questions them. Questions relate to the facilitator's aims – for a greater understanding of an individual the questions would be about how they feel, how they are being treated, what changes they would like from the groups, etc. This method is also useful when the role-play is stuck over an undisclosed piece of information. As facilitator you can question the characters in role and try to get that piece of information out into the open.

Modelling and demonstrating   The facilitator stops the role-play, moves in as one of the characters and shows another way of tackling the situation. This is a tricky method to use. It can result in role-players feeling undermined by the facilitator. It can, however, be used to good effect with an experienced group who know that this kind of intervention may occur. For the facilitator, it is an effective way of moving the role-play forward very quickly. To enhance group involvement, observers can also be given the opportunity to step in and change the action.

Suggesting and directing   The facilitator stops the action, gives a direction and immediately moves out again. This is useful if the facilitator perceives that a player is straying from their given task. (It should be done sensitively, however, so as not to undermine their efforts.) It can also be used to speed up a process. The facilitator could give a direction which will force the group to come to a quick decision. (For example: 'The officials are about to arrive – you have two minutes to come to a decision!') The facilitator can also use this method without stopping the action, by quietly whispering instructions into the ear of an individual.

All these methods require a ritual way of stopping action and restarting it. One commonly accepted way is to say 'freeze' or 'stop'. It is important to have an agreed word to use so that stopping the action is clean and clear. A messy stop in the middle of a role-play can throw everyone off balance.

Processing

Debriefing

Hot-seating is an option. The characters remain in role at the end of the role-play, and are asked questions to which they respond in character. Use this technique to find out more about what was going on in the role-play and how in-role characters felt about it.

De-roling is an important stage before moving on to evaluation. It involves the player finishing off the role and officially coming out of it, with a very clear distinction between the role and the player, the 'mask' and the face. Give each character an opportunity to say anything else they need to in role. Then take off the in-role name tag and welcome the individual back. Then give the individual an opportunity to say anything they like to the character they were playing. (The player speaks to an empty chair which represents the character they were playing.) This helps the player to come out of role.

Evaluation

Questions for the group For example: Were the instructions clear? Was the facilitation helpful? What did you learn from the role-play?

Questions for the facilitator For example: Did the group stick to the focus? Were individuals following instructions? Were the aims of the role-play met?

If there were major problems in the role-play, ask the role-players questions about their difficulties so that they have an opportunity to find solutions. Remember, though, that debriefing must come before evaluation. The two processes must not be confused. Participants should have been allowed to leave their roles behind before being asked to discuss what did or did not work.

Group dynamics: games, exercises and discussion tools

Icebreakers

GAMES and exercises to introduce people to each other, and break down initial inhibitions, for use when a group first meets.

Throwing a name

You will need two or three small beanbags. (Balls will do.) Everyone stands in a circle. Begin with one beanbag. The bag is thrown round the circle randomly. Each time it is caught the catcher says their own name. Keep this going until everyone has had a go. Now ask participants to call the name of the person to whom they are throwing as well, and keep this going until everyone has had a go.

In the next round participants stop saying their own names as they catch, but continue to say the name of the person to whom they are throwing. Everyone is thrown the bag just once. When the round is completed, repeat it in exactly the same sequence. Each person has only to remember who they threw to last time. Half-way through this round introduce another bag, to be thrown in exactly the same sequence. You can continue adding another bag. The game can be further extended by having everyone move out of the circle and walk round the room. Participants must now be even more aware from whom they receive and to whom they throw, while continuing the same sequence.

Adjective names

Sitting in a circle everyone introduces themselves one after the other, prefixing their name with an adjective which says something good about themselves. It can be as outrageously positive as they like – Superb Sabir, Fantastic Fred, Animated Annie, or whatever. The second person repeats the first person's name and adjective and adds their own. The third person repeats the previous two, adding their own. And so on. The person who is last has the hardest job!

Animal names

Follow the same format as *Adjective names*, but this time each person chooses an animal beginning with the same letter or sound as their name, instead of giving an adjective: 'I'm Peter the penguin', 'I'm Jackie the jaguar', or whatever. Each person repeats the name and animal of the people before them, and adds their own. A variation on this is for participants to choose an animal they would like to be and say why: 'I'm Fiona the cheetah because . . . ' The person next to them then says: 'This is Fiona the cheetah. I'm Roger the fox because . . . ' Participants could also devise a physical gesture or pose for each of the animals.

The sun shines on

Everyone sits on chairs in a circle. One person stands in the middle. The aim of the game is for the person in the middle to get a chair to sit in. They state something that is true of themselves, and if it is also true of anyone else in the circle they must move seats. The statement always begins with the phrase 'The sun shines on everyone who ...'

The game can begin with visual observations ('The sun shines on everyone who is wearing trainers') and move on to statements about more private matters, such as personal likes and dislikes ('The sun shines on everyone who likes swimming in the sea') or even political convictions.

Mingle and grab

Everyone walks round the room, greeting. They move fast or slow depending on what the leader wants. Every few minutes call out a number. Participants get into groups of whatever that number is and hold on to each other in a hug. If the number called is one, participants stand still and hug themselves. It is good to call the number of the whole group at the end, so that everyone huddles as one group.

Shake all hands

Everyone in the room shakes everyone else's hand within a strict time limit of one minute. This gets energy up, and obliges each participant to acknowledge everyone else.

Touch these things

This is a race to see how quickly participants can touch four or five named objects. Call out a short list of things in the room,

such as a hard chair, a windowsill, someone's trouser-leg, something red, and a light switch. Participants touch them as quickly as they can, not necessarily in that order. The last person to finish can call out the next list.

Find your noise

Participants get into pairs and agree on a noise that they can make and recognise. One half of each pair stands on one side of the room, and the other half on the opposite side. Everyone closes their eyes and finds their partner by using their noise. This is a good exercise for encouraging concentration and listening, and creating a bond between the pairs.

Body rub

A quick physical exercise to get participants moving and greeting each other. The leader calls out 'rub', and everyone turns to someone and chooses (within reason) a part of their body to rub – shoulder, knee or thigh, perhaps. As they rub, they say 'shoulder rub, shoulder rub, shoulder rub' or whatever, according to which part of the body they are rubbing. The facilitator shouts 'change', and everyone finds a new person and a different part of the body to rub. The exercise continues as above.

Find your shoes

Everyone takes off their shoes and puts them in the middle of the room. The leader muddles all the shoes around and retreats to the side of the room. Put a time limit on the next stage, depending on how many there are in the group. (A group of twenty should have only 30 seconds.) When the facilitator calls, participants must find and put on their shoes within the time limit. The more people, the better the game is. If the group is small, have them do the exercise blindfold.

Warm-ups and lighteners

These are some of the most popular games and exercises of their kind. Choose those which you feel fit in with what is needed.

Equidistant noses

Everyone silently chooses two people in the room. When the leader gives the call, participants have to get themselves between the two they have chosen, with the aim of keeping their own nose an equal distance from the other two. Encourage people to use the whole space. There are variations on this game:

Variation 1 When choosing their two people, participants choose a person they want to get as close as possible to and a person they want to get as far away from as possible.

Variation 2 One of the two people they choose is a bomb which is going to blow them up, the other a shield which can protect them. They aim to keep the shield between themselves and the bomb.

Kiss and bite

Stand in a circle. Turn to the person on your right and tell them something visual that you like about them (either something they are wearing or – within reason – a physical attribute). Then turn to the person on your left and tell them something you don't like about them (again it must be something you can see). When the whole group have done this, they bite whatever they said they like and they kiss whatever they said they don't like. This game is great for getting the laughs going, but can really only be used once with a group of people: when they know the game they can plan to make it easier for themselves, and of course the element of surprise is lost.

Fast-motion film

In groups of three decide on a film you all know. You have three minutes to condense the main themes of the film into a one-minute performance. When the three minutes are up, the performances are viewed one at a time and the audience tries to identify the film.

Back-to-back mirror

In pairs stand back-to-back, or sit on the floor back-to-back. It is important that partners are touching from the base of the spine to the head. Decide who will lead in each pair. The leader begins very slowly moving those parts of their body which are in contact with their partner. Their partner mirrors them through what they can feel. There should be no spoken communication. The partners swap over, so that each has an opportunity to be leader and to be led.

Mirroring in pairs

In pairs, players stand opposite each other. One partner makes movements; the other mirrors them. You can play this either with one part of the body touching (perhaps two fingertips) or with no physical contact at all. If the two partners are touching, one can lead the other around the room. Swap over so that each person has a go at leading.

Group mirroring

To begin with, have everyone working as one large group. Decide on a leader. Stand in a circle and mirror the leader's gestures as closely as possible. Try to get to the stage where an outsider would not be able to tell who the leader is. (This is a variation on the game in which someone leaves the room, a leader is decided in their absence, and when they return they have to guess who it is.)

Grandmother's keys

This is an adaptation of an old children's game. One person volunteers to be the grandmother. The grandmother stands at the end of the room looking towards the wall with her back to the rest. Behind her, at her feet, is a large jangly set of keys. The rest of the group move towards her slowly. Every time she turns round they freeze. If she sees anyone move they have to go back to the beginning. She gives no warning as to when she will turn round. The aim of the group is to retrieve the keys and get them back to the start without the grandmother seeing them. Once the keys have been grabbed each person has to touch them on their journey back to the beginning. If anyone is caught with them, the keys are returned to grandmother and the participant goes back to the beginning. A group will soon realise that the only way to achieve their aim is to work together and make sure that every time the grandmother turns around she is not able to tell who has the keys.

Mime the lie

Stand round in a circle. One by one everyone goes into the middle of the circle and mimes an action, such as mowing the lawn. The next person asks them what they are doing. They lie and say, for example, 'I'm feeding the dog.' The person who asked now goes into the circle and mimes whatever the previous person said. When they are asked what they are doing they again lie, and so the game continues.

My bonnie lies over the ocean

This exercise is based around the song. Stand in a circle and sing it through to check that everyone knows it. Now when you sing it everyone bobs down when they hear a word start with a 'b', and bobs up again at the next one.

Number everyone in the group 1 or 2. Now when you sing, the twos start off standing and the ones start off bobbed down; so on the first 'b' the ones bob up and the twos bob down; and so on.

The snake game

One participant, volunteering to be the snake, is blindfolded and led to the centre of the room. The other participants agree to keep their eyes closed. Both the snake and the other participants can move wherever they want to in the room. The snake must keep hissing at all times. The snake has to catch as many people as possible. When caught, the person dies as loudly and dramatically as they like. They can then open their eyes and help the facilitator by watching for anyone about to bump into walls or furniture. (It is a good idea to start the game off with a few people staying out of the action and making sure that participants do not hurt themselves.) This is an excellent game for encouraging concentration and listening.

Trust games

All these games are about building up group trust, awareness, co-operation and confidence, and demand extreme concentration. They should be introduced and facilitated with the utmost care, so that participants are fully aware what they are about. Care with the safety of participants is paramount.

Wind in the willows

Gather round in a tight circle. One person volunteers to go in the middle. They close their eyes and allow themselves to fall, keeping their body straight, and the others catch and support them. (Supporters hold hands up in front and stand with one leg slightly in front of the other with knees bent. This is the strongest possible position.) Initially the group should have their hands close to the middle so that the person need not feel they are falling far. As confidence grows, the people in the group can move away a little. Take turns and give everyone the opportunity to have a go. Take care that there are plenty of people able to hold someone up, specially if there is a heavier person in the middle.

Running blindfold

Stand all the participants at one end of the room. One person volunteers to be blindfold and stands at the other end of the room. They run to the end where the group are standing. The group must be prepared to catch the running person gently. They should stand in a half-moon shape, and shout stop before the runner reaches them. Initially people anticipate reaching the end of the room, and begin to slow down. Encourage people to run as fast as they can until the group shouts stop, and to trust that the group will really make sure they don't hit the wall.

Walking blindfold

Everyone stands in a large circle. One person volunteers to be blindfold and is taken to the middle of the circle. From there they can walk in any direction, and when they get to the edge of the circle the nearest person gently takes hold of them and redirects them. Make sure there is time for everyone to have a turn at being blindfold.

Where shall we go?

Participants divide into pairs. One person in each pair is blindfold. The seeing person asks them where they would like to go. This can be anywhere from a beach to a fairground or a party. It is entirely up to the person who is blindfold. The seeing person holds them by the hand or arm and takes them on a walk round the room, guiding them physically through the imaginary landscape. It is up to the seeing person to describe exactly where they are and what they are doing.

Through the rushes

Participants stand in two lines facing each other, far enough apart for their outstretched arms to meet and slightly overlap. One by one each participant moves to one end, closes their eyes and walks between the two lines. The person moving through should have to push very slightly against the outstretched arms. It can be a very relaxing sensation.

Pass round the room

A volunteer lies on the ground and closes their eyes. The rest of the group lift them up above their heads and walk round the room with them. If there are enough people in the group, the person could be passed from one group to another. Give as many people as possible a turn to be carried.

Hands

In pairs spend five minutes observing each other's hands. Hold them, feel them and look at them. Feel them with your eyes closed. Join up with several other pairs. One person closes their eyes and tries to find their partner's hands. Have a turn at this one by one.

Count to twenty

Sit in a circle and close your eyes. The group aims to count to 20 without deciding who says which number. Every time two people say the number at the same time you go back to the beginning again. It is actually easier to do with your eyes closed, but if a group wants to start with their eyes open they may find they can make it work that way. Having extra rules can make it easier to start with (for instance, that each person is allowed to say only one number). As the group gets better at it, take away these rules and the group can find great satisfaction in succeeding.

Tropical rainstorm

Everyone stands in a circle. The facilitator begins the storm by rubbing their hands together. One by one, everyone copies the person to their right. Each individual does only what the person on their right does, regardless of what the facilitator is doing. The facilitator moves from rubbing hands, to clicking their fingers, to clapping, to slapping their thighs, to stamping their feet. The storm abates in the opposite way to which it began – that is, from stamping and slapping to clapping, clicking and rubbing. The round ends with silence.

Mental gifts

Sit in a circle. One by one each person announces that they are giving a gift to the person on their left – for example, 'I give you the gift of believing in your own strength.' Try to make the gift appropriate to the recipient, reflecting something you have learnt about them during the session. This is not a good exercise to do until the group has done some challenging work together.

Group discussion techniques

Whip round

Description   A group listening exercise with input from each participant.

Aims   To allow opportunity for feelings, grievances or needs to be expressed and heard without judgment or criticism. To allow for full participation.

Directions   (1) Everyone sits in a circle. The trainer introduces the subject – for example, an observation or a thought about the session or day to leave us all with. (2) Taking turns in a clockwise motion, each participant makes their offering. The others listen without comment. This is not an opportunity for participants to make long statements. It is a quick gathering of points of view or observations. There is no discussion.

Notes   Whatever a person chooses to offer is valid – there is no space for judgment. This can be a useful way of ending things each day. If practised regularly, it can become a sustaining influence in a group. It is an affirmative and supportive practice, allowing people to express their feelings without questioning or judgment.

Skills   Listening. Expression. Participation.

The bracelet

Description   A group discussion structure providing an opportunity for participants to make contributions without pressure. For use when talking about a difficult subject.

Aims   To provide a safe environment in which feelings and emotions can be communicated.

Directions   (1) You will need an attractive and fairly substantial object: for example, a thick bracelet, a stone or a paperweight. Gather the group round in a circle, and place the object in the middle. Introduce the exercise as group listening. If there is a particular conflict the group is involved in, introduce the exercise as a preliminary to talking about the conflict – as a chance for people to express their needs and fears without being pushed into argument about it. (2) The object is the key which unlocks each person's opportunity to speak. When someone wants to say how they feel about the issue under discussion, they must go to the centre of the circle,

pick up the object, and return to their seat before they can speak. Once someone has the object in their hands, they can speak for as long as they like, and can say as much or as little as they wish, although individuals are also responsible for noticing how much of the allotted time they are taking up. The speaker returns the object to the middle when they have finished speaking. (3) Members of the group can keep an eye out for anyone who wants to speak. Everyone should have a turn to hold the object. If they do not wish to speak while holding it, they need not do so; but by holding it and maintaining the right to silence, they are claiming the time, space and attention that those who want to speak have had.

Notes   There should be no comeback from anyone once a point has been made. People have a right to express how they feel and are under no obligation to justify it. Individuals can respond to what someone else has said, but not by dismissing or rubbishing it. The exercise is not an opportunity for people to insult one another while knowing that retaliation is not allowed. If a group is volatile it can be a remarkable quietener, and when used sensitively by a group it is an excellent exercise. The participants have to be sensitive to each other's needs, restraining themselves if they are used to talking, and pushing themselves if they are not.

Skills   Listening. Patience. Participation.

Gathering

Description   A discussion structure which allows the group to share values, thoughts and opinions in a non-threatening environment.

Aims   To build group cohesion. To explore a range of opinions within the group.

Directions   (1) Ask a key question to the whole group. For example: What qualities do you value in a friend? What do you want your children to learn from you? What is one of the things you like most about yourself? (2) Each participant responds individually in turn.

Notes   This can be an excellent way of bringing the group together at the beginning of each session or day. It is also a useful way of building trust within the group through the sharing of personal information.

Skills   Openness. Honesty. Communication.

The inner circle

Description   A structured group discussion technique to facilitate the exchanging of ideas.

Aims   To provide a sound framework in which an ordered discussion can take place. To facilitate a process in which all can participate. To facilitate a process in which the focus is on the speaker.

Directions   (1) Place three chairs in the middle of the circle. Once the topic for discussion has been identified, participants are invited to fill the three chairs. The chairs don't all have to be filled to start the discussion. (2) Only the participants in the three chairs in the middle may speak. Each may do so twice at most, for no longer than three minutes at a time. They may speak for the second time only when the other two participants in the middle have spoken at least once. Having spoken twice, they vacate their chair and return to the outer circle of observing participants. (3) If a participant in the outer circle wishes to speak, they can tap one of the three seated participants on the shoulder, who will then vacate their chair. But they should only approach someone who has spoken at least once. (4) If a participant who has already had a turn in the middle wishes to re-enter and speak again, they may do so only when everyone has had an opportunity in the middle. The facilitator can decide when it is appropriate to end the discussion. (It is good to ask the group if they feel they have fully explored the topic.)

Notes   Those speaking in the middle of the circle should address all conversation to the other seated participants. No comments should be personally directed. Someone in the group should be appointed timekeeper and adjudicator, monitoring the frequency of speakers' contributions. This is an especially good technique to use when sensitive or provocative issues are being discussed. Members need to concentrate on the discussion in order to choose the appropriate time to enter the middle and make their contribution.

Skills   Clarity. Listening. Observation. Concentration. Self-control. Communication.

Resources

Books

Ways and Means: the handbook of the Kingston Friends Workshop Group
ISBN 0 9510821 0 8

A practical handbook compiled for those living or working with children. Although all the exercises are written with children in mind, many of them can be successfully used with adults with little or no adaptation. A good introduction to the idea of peaceful problem-solving. Available on request from Kingston Friends Workshop Group (see *Organisations*).

Creative Conflict Resolution
William Kreidler
Scott, Foresman and Co., ISBN 0 637 15642 7

A book for use with older children, packed with practical ideas and exercises which have been tested in schools. The materials cover ten areas, ranging from helping students handle anger, frustration and aggression, to teaching tolerance.

Getting to Yes
Roger Fisher and William Ury (Harvard Negotiating Project)
Penguin, ISBN 0 0916 4071 7

An informative book on the art of negotiating. It outlines the skills needed for successful negotiating, and offers ideas to encourage the reader to practise these skills. It treats negotiation as an everyday activity that we are all involved in, and which we can become more successful at with practice. This is helpful background reading for understanding what makes good listening and mediating.

A Woman in Your Own Right: assertiveness and you
Anne Dickson
Quartet, ISBN 0 7043 3420 8

A highly practical book with pages full of analysis and ideas. Positive and supportive, the book encourages us to look at ourselves and learn to live with what we see. Dickson describes four familiar types of behaviour, each of which is represented by a character in the book. One of them represents the assertive person in each of us. The book leads the reader towards an understanding of how we can develop this potential in ourselves. Primarily aimed at women but a helpful book for anyone, offering a clear view of what assertiveness is all about.

Everyone Can Win

Helena Cornelius and Shoshana Faire

Simon and Schuster, ISBN 0 7318 0111 3

A book for anyone who would like to acquire more skills for dealing with conflict. It shows how to recognise typical conflict patterns and how to avoid them. It teaches how to understand the power dynamics in any relationship. Full of case studies and stories which illustrate how different individuals have responded to conflict, ranging from minor discomforts to serious confrontations. An inspirational source book for all those interested in learning how to win.

The Magic of Conflict

Thomas F. Crum

Simon and Schuster, ISBN 0 6716 6836 6

A wonderful book, full of stories and sayings. Easy to read, but perhaps not immediately practical. Crum relates his own experiences of aggression and conflict to the wider context of his social environment. His philosophy and his faith are inspiring, and the book includes good ideas about coping with stress and conflict. But his way is a way of life – not something that can be learnt overnight.

See under Organisations for details of where to obtain these books.

Organisations

Alternatives to Violence Project (AVP)

15 Rutherford Place, New York, NY 10003, USA

Tel: 0101–212 477 1067

AVP runs workshops in prisons and in the community, exploring alternatives to violence in a unique project which is facilitated by inmates and outside volunteers together. AVP UK can be contacted through Pam Hughes (QSRE), Friends House, Euston Road, London NW1 2BJ. Tel: 071 387 3601.

Community Board Programme, Inc.

149 Ninth Street, San Francisco, CA 94103, USA

Tel: 0101 415 552 1250

This project has compiled a mediators' manual and a secondary school curriculum for conflict resolution, both of which can be obtained directly from them.

Conflict Resolution Network

Box 1016 Chatswood, NSW, 2057, Australia

Tel: 010–61(02) 419 8500

The Conflict Resolution Network is a peace programme of the United Nations Association of Australia. It is a national campaign to develop, teach and learn conflict resolution skills for personal and professional effectiveness. It has published an eight-session conflict resolution course, a source book entitled *Everyone Can Win* (see the book list) and a series of interviews and discussions on audio tape. All of these are available from the above address.

Mediation UK

82A Gloucester Road, Bishopston, Bristol BS7 8BN

Tel: 0272 241234

Mediation UK is the umbrella organisation for all the mediation and reparation schemes in the UK. A complete list of all the mediation centres in the country is available from them on request.

Forum Bookshop

86 Abbey Street, Derby DE3 3SQ

Tel: 0332 368039

Forum stocks a wide range of conflict resolution materials, and will order books not in stock.

Geese Theatre Company

220 Moseley Road, Highgate, Birmingham B12 0DG

Tel: 021 446 4370

Geese performs plays and runs workshops in prisons and the probation service, with a focus on changing offenders' destructive patterns of behaviour. It is available for running training workshops on this theme.

Kingston Friends Workshop Group

78 Eden Street, Kingston upon Thames, Surrey KT1 1DJ

Tel: 081 547 1197

Kingston Friends runs conflict resolution workshops in schools for adults and children. Its handbook, *Ways and Means* (see the book list), is available on request.

Leap Confronting Conflict

Leaveners Arts Base, 8 Lennox Road, Finsbury Park, London N4 3NW

Tel: 071 272 5630

Leap Confronting Conflict runs training courses and workshops throughout the country, with young people and those who work with them, on various aspects of everyday group and personal conflicts.

Red Ladder Theatre Company

Cobden Avenue, Lower Wortley, Leeds LS12 5PB

Tel: 0532 792228

Red Ladder works specifically for the youth service, performing shows and running workshops throughout the country. It is constantly devising new material in response to requests.

REDO (Jacque Price Rees and Bernadette Dolan)

25 Roderick Road, Hampstead, London NW3 2NN

Tel: 081 485 0659

REDO runs workshops and courses in the physical art of non-aggressive self-defence.

School Mediation Associates (SMA)

702 Green St, Apartment 8, Cambridge, MA 02139, USA

SMA has produced an excellent manual for use with young people who are being trained as mediators. The material is designed for use with those aged 11 years upwards.

Youth at Risk USA

The Breakthrough Foundation, 3059 Fillmore Street, San Francisco, CA 94123, USA

Tel: 0101 415 673 0171

Youth at Risk runs intensive residential projects and community programmes with inner-city young people at risk throughout the USA. There is a group in the UK working on setting up similar projects here. Contact Ben Rose, Youth at Risk UK, Central Administration Unit, Bovingdon, Marlow Common, Bucks SL7 2QR. Tel: 071 383 3839.

THE FUEL

Ourselves and our communication

THE FUEL

Ourselves and our communication

The raw material of the fire lies still. Piles of dead wood and scattered coals cover the earth. The dead dry wood is highly combustible; the coals can withstand heat a little longer. Some of the wood is still damp, and flame-resistant to some degree; the treated wood is highly resistant. The raw materials of fire are constantly changing: dead wood disintegrates, new wood grows, coals form, and all is movement. The raw material of fire lies still but alive.

THERE is potential for conflict within us and around us all the time. Life and conflict are inextricably linked. Conflict is part of life and growth. Without conflict there would be no change and no challenge. Where energies meet there is movement and potential opposition, challenge and change.

By building an awareness of ourselves and those around us as fuel for violent conflict, we can discover productive alternatives to a damaging blaze. There is creative potential in conflict, just as there is potential in fire for warmth and energy as well as destruction. Developing self-awareness and communication skills is a way of working on the potential for challenge and growth in conflict, rather than allowing it to fester through lack of attention and awareness.

Focus   People as the fuel for conflict: personal perceptions of and assumptions about others; how people communicate; personal histories.

Aims   To examine the relationship between personal history and the way we respond to situations of conflict. To practise skills of clear and direct communication. To examine to what extent our knowledge of others determines the effectiveness of our responses in times of conflict.

Key concepts   Communication: receiving, understanding, listening, expression. Awareness: personal histories, self-awareness, awareness of others.

Key questions   To what extent does self-awareness determine our response in situations of conflict? How do our overall communication skills relate to our behaviour in conflict situations? To what extent does our understanding of others determine how successful we are when attempting to resolve conflict?

This section contains three two-and-a-half-hour sessions. Session 1 deals with a definition of conflict, our responses to situations of conflict, and asssumptions and attitudes. Session 2 deals with personal history, characteristics of effective communication, and different ways of listening. Session 3 focuses on communication skills, body language and interpretation, clear expression, and the dynamics of receiving.

All training techniques (such as brainstorm, role-play and tableau work) are explained in TRAINING FOR TRAINERS.

Session 1

Introduction Introduction to the facilitators and the training centre; outline of the course; structure of the course; timetable; questions; and participants introduce themselves. (See *INTRODUCTION* and *TRAINING FOR TRAINERS*.) *30 min.*

1.1 LETTER TO AN ALIEN: CONFLICT IS . . . ? *35 min.*
1.2 CONFLICT: WHAT DO YOU DO? *30 min.*
1.3 PUNCHY PROVERBS *30 min.*

Introduction to fuel: people as the raw material for conflict
5 min.

1.4 FIXED POSITIONS *10 min.*
1.5 INSTANT GUESSING *15 min.*
1.6 LIKES AND DISLIKES *15 min.*
1.7 WHERE DO YOU STAND? *15 min.*

Reflection *10 min.*

Notes The first three exercises introduce themes which run through the entire course. We would recommend doing Exercise 1.1 and then choosing either 1.2 or 1.3. The other four exercises serve as introductions to the idea of people as 'fuel' for conflict. Exercises 1.4 and 1.5 deal with how we make assumptions and judgments about other people. We suggest both are done. Exercises 1.6 and 1.7 deal with our own attitudes and concerns. We suggest that one of these is chosen. Session 1 would therefore consist of five practical exercises plus introductions and reflection.

Exercise 1.1 *Time: 35 min.*

LETTER TO AN ALIEN: CONFLICT IS ... ?

Description A large-group exercise exploring the meaning of the word *conflict*.

Aims To clarify what we mean by conflict. To discover the range of responses within the group. To work towards a group definition of conflict.

Directions

1 Divide a large sheet of paper into columns, each headed by a letter of the alphabet. For the purposes of this exercise choose letters A to H.

2 Ask participants individually to brainstorm conflict words. Each should try to provide at least one word for each letter (for example, A–anger, B–broken . . .). The words can be written down by a nominated scribe as they are called out, or simply added to the chart by each individual participant. There is no debate or questioning at this stage about why certain words have been chosen. *5 min.*

3 Once the chart is completed (it's good to have a strict time limit), people can ask each other questions about their chosen words – what certain words mean, how they are connected with conflict, and so forth. But no judgments are to be passed. *3 min.*

4 Participants split into pairs or groups of three and select a letter from the chart. (It is best if each pair or group has a different letter.) They then draft a short communication to an extraterrestrial alien who has never heard of conflict, explaining what it is. Each group should use the words listed under their letter. The communications are then shared with the whole group. *10 min.*

5 Mixing participants into new groups of four or five, ask each group to create a brief definition of conflict in the form of a slogan. These could all start with 'Conflict is . . .' Then let each group try to think of an imaginative way to present their definition. They could use tableaux, involving everyone in the presentation. Extra time will be needed if a presentation is to be prepared. *10 min.*

Exercise 1.1 *Continued*

Feedback and discussion Back in the whole group, participants are invited to reflect individually on their experience of interaction between group members. How did the group draft its letter to the alien? How did the group agree upon its definition? (Were they surprised by anyone else's definition?) Was it easy to get to a slogan on conflict? There are other questions that might be asked. Have they learnt anything about conflict from this exercise? Are they clearer now? Do they feel that any crucial aspect has been missed out?   *7 min.*

Notes Participants could be invited to develop their definitions of conflict over the period of the whole course. These should evolve as the subject is explored in greater depth. It would be valuable, at the end of the course, to see if the whole group could agree on a final common definition.

Skills Literacy. Group interaction. Group devising.

Exercise 1.2 *Time: 30 min.*

CONFLICT: WHAT DO YOU DO?

Description A group writing exercise exploring responses to conflict.

Aims To gain an insight into the wide variety of responses within the group. To share these responses. To make connections between the responses.

Directions

1 Invite the group to consider one of the following questions or some combination of them: What are your usual responses to situations of conflict? Have you got different ways of responding according to circumstances? What feelings do you experience in situations of conflict? Ask every participant to do a personal brainstorm on their own piece of paper. Ask them to write down what immediately comes to mind – no censorship or over-thoughtfulness, just spontaneous response. It might be helpful for participants to think of specific situations and how they actually responded to them.   *10 min.*

2 Ask participants to read their list aloud one by one, sitting in a circle. Then invite comments. (An alternative is for every participant to read just one word at a time, repeatedly going round the circle.)   *10 min.*

Feedback and discussion Are there common responses? Are there any patterns emerging? (Are there, for instance, any responses which seem to be specific to male or female, black or white, members of the group?) Why do we respond in the way that we do? What are the most common responses? What are the least common? Do people think of conflict as something intrapersonal, interpersonal, intra-group, or inter-group? Is there any positive response to conflict in the group? Is there potential to look at conflict as a positive force for change?   *10 min.*

Notes This is a good way to gain everyone's involvement. It is also a structured way of acquiring information. Participants do not need to be highly articulate. Brainstorming sometimes by-passes inhibitions that people might have if asked to express themselves generally on a difficult subject. Most people find it easy to respond in single words or short phrases.

Skills Group interaction.

Exercise 1.3   *Time: 30 min.*

PUNCHY PROVERBS

Description   A small-group exercise exploring the effects of violence and violent behaviour.

Aims   To generate debate on the use of violence against others and its effects. To encourage the group to express their personal opinions on the subject. To involve the group in bringing to life a proverb.

Directions

1   Divide the participants into groups of three or four. Using cards prepared in advance, give each group a proverb that deals with some aspect of violent behaviour. Add your own discoveries to these two African examples:

When two elephants fight, it is the grass that suffers most.

The axe forgets; the log does not.

2   Each group works out an interpretation of its proverb. What does it mean to them? What circumstances might it be referring to? Can the group think of concrete situations? The results of small-group work are then fed back to the whole group. If the small group is unanimous in its understanding, then one member could feed back. If it is not, the group must decide who says what. It is valuable at this stage to see the variety of interpretations and responses.   *10 min.*

3   The small groups are now asked to choose a way of visualising their proverb, as a tableau (frozen image) or a series of tableaux.   *10 min.*

4   Invite each group to exhibit its tableau to the whole group. Ask each figure in the frozen image to say what it is feeling or thinking. Participants observing the tableaux explore what they see and guess at what the proverb could be before the text is shared.
If there is time, this tableau could now be developed into a short dramatic scene which might deepen everyone's understanding of the proverb.   *5 min.*

Feedback and discussion   Do the group know any other proverbs or sayings which refer to situations of violence or conflict? You might suggest that they ask friends, parents, grandparents, or people in the community from different cultural backgrounds for any relevant sayings or proverbs, and then display these on the walls over future sessions.   *5 min.*

Notes   Participants could decide to develop their own sayings. These might be worked on and shared over later weeks or months. It could be useful to look at a variety of sayings dealing with different issues related to the course's themes. Discussion of the origins of such sayings can be valuable. Is there stored wisdom or stored prejudice here? Do the sayings need to be challenged? You might find it necessary to explore and discuss some of the issues raised in the tableaux or dramatic scenes, especially those to do with violence or conflict in the family.

Skills   Interpretation. Dialogue. Imagination. Dramatising. Teamwork.

Exercise 1.4   *Time: 10 min.*

FIXED POSITIONS

Description   A quick group exercise to examine the relationship between attitudes, perceptions and background, and to provide a stimulus for discussion.

Aims   To examine the possibility that what we perceive depends on our perspective. To promote discussion on how our backgrounds, and our lack of knowledge or experience of a situation, could influence our response to it.

Directions

1   Form a circle and ask one group member to stand in the middle. Ask someone standing in front of the person in the middle, 'How many eyes have they got?' Ask someone standing behind the person in the middle the same question. Ask someone standing directly to the side of the person in the middle the same question. The person in the middle stands still, facing the same way throughout the questions and answers. At all times participants answer according to what they can actually *see* from their static position, not what they *know* is there. The answers will be two, none, and one, respectively.   *5 min.*

2   You can then follow the same procedure with another member in the middle and choosing, say, the arms this time.

Feedback and discussion   How does your perspective on a situation shape your understanding of it? How can we give ourselves a more complete picture more of the time? In what way can you relate this exercise to your everyday experience?
                                                                    5 min.

Notes   What happens if we get an opportunity to walk round the circle and perceive the person in the middle from all angles? It is a good idea to have a participant try it, and to ask them to give a running commentary on what they are seeing and how their vision of the person changes. The everyday analysis of this can also be developed in discussion. You could place a member at the other end of the room and ask them to walk slowly towards the rest of the group. How does distance influence what detail can be observed?

Skills   Observation.

Exercise 1.5   *Time: 15 min.*

INSTANT GUESSING

Description   A quick introductory exercise in pairs, exploring the assumptions we make about each other.

Aims   To examine the basis on which we make assumptions about other people. To introduce a discussion about our prejudices.

Directions

1   Each participant finds a partner. The facilitator asks a question: 'Does your partner take sugar in their tea or coffee?' Both partners guess and give their answer to each other. They tell each other whether they were right or wrong. At this stage they can tell each other briefly why they thought what they did.   *10 min.*

2   Partners now change. Another question is asked. This process is repeated several times, each time with a new partner. The questions can be made more personal in nature. For example: What party does your partner vote for? Is your partner married? Does your partner have a mortgage? How old is your partner? What job do they do? What music or literature do they like? Do they own a car? What are their hobbies or interests?

Feedback and discussion   Participants can reflect on how many times they were right or wrong. How did they come to the conclusions they came to? On the basis of what outward clues did they make their assumptions? Did those clues lead them to correct or incorrect assumptions? These questions can then be related to how we make assumptions about people on first meeting. If we base those assumptions on things like appearance, age, sex, race, fashion, and so forth, how far does prejudice lie at the root of what we assume?   *5 min.*

Notes   This exercise should be snappy and game-like. (It is a good icebreaker.) The tone should not be judgmental in any way but should focus on the assumptions made rather than the person about whom they are made. It could also be used to look at a particular subject area – for example, what we assume from physical appearances.

Skills   Quick decision-making.

Exercise 1.6 *Time: 15 min.*

LIKES AND DISLIKES

Description A quick group exercise in which participants give immediate expression to their likes and dislikes.

Aims To determine quickly the feelings of the group. To see if any trends emerge.

Directions

1 Place ten chairs in a straight line. Give each chair a number from 1 to 10 consecutively. Ask the group your first question: for example, 'Do you enjoy using public transport?' Participants indicate their answer by placing themselves in front of the appropriate chair. In this case, no. 1 would be the chair to choose if you absolutely loved the public transport system; no. 10 would be your choice if you absolutely hated it; and a chair in the middle would indicate that you were undecided, really didn't know, or had no strong feelings for or against.   *10 min.*

2 Follow the same procedure with other questions. The questions should become more personal or challenging: Are you a vegetarian? Do you feel hanging should be reintroduced? Could you be a pacifist?

Feedback and discussion What patterns emerged during the exercise? Did you notice any differences between the likes and dislikes of the men and the women in the group? What influences our likes and dislikes?   *5 min.*

Notes The same exercise can be used for other purposes. For example, the questions could be designed to gauge what situations members of the group find most difficult to deal with. No. 1 chair could be the 'easy' position and no. 10 the most 'difficult'. You could use the same structure to find out what makes participants most angry. In each case you can look out for patterns emerging within the group. These could be the subject of interesting and stimulating discussion.

Skills Quick decision-making. Observation of the group. Being aware of one's own feelings.

Exercise 1.7 *Time: 15 min.*

WHERE DO YOU STAND?

Description A group exercise in which individual participants have to take a stand on a specific issue.

Aims To determine the range of feelings within the group relating to various issues. To locate the areas of difference or the degree of consensus within the group.

Directions

1 Designate three areas of the room: one end is the 'for' position; the other end is 'against'; a line in the middle of the room is the 'neutral' or 'sitting on the fence' position.

2 Call out the first theme or issue: 'Where do you stand on the reintroduction of the death penalty?' Participants take up positions which reflect their response to the question. *10 min.*

3 Repeat the exercise by asking further questions, or explore the first issue further (see the notes).

Feedback and discussion Having presented them with a range of issues, ask the group if they could see any patterns of response. Were members equally divided? How often was the neutral position being used? How easy was it to take a clear stand for or against? Did they feel better in the outside positions or the middle position? How did they feel about having to make up their mind so quickly? Were there any issues they felt they needed to know more about? Were they at all surprised at how the group subdivided during the exercise? How does this exercise relate to the real world?   *5 min.*

Notes This exercise can be useful for exploring one issue in depth – the death penalty, for instance. The three groups that emerge can work separately, exploring through discussion why they have chosen their specific position. They might be surprised to see how many different reasons and motivations emerge. Each group could then feed back all their different reasons to the other groups, perhaps using role-play or tableau presentation. The groups could then discuss their understanding of each other's positions. More time needs to be allocated for this.

Skills Quick decision-making. Observation of the group. Being aware of one's own opinions and beliefs.

Session 2

Notes   Exercises 2.8 and 2.9 are further introductions to the 'fuel' idea, focusing on the course participants themselves and allowing them to share information about their lives. We suggest one is chosen. Exercise 2.10 is a large-group exercise examining communication. Exercises 2.11 and 2.12 are both listening exercises. We suggest one is chosen. Exercise 2.13 is an active listening exercise. Exercise 2.14 is a group co-operation and listening exercise which is suggested to close the session. Session 2 should include five practical exercises along with the introduction and reflection.

Exercise 2.8   *Time: 40 min.*

PERSONAL HISTORIES

Description   Individual and group work enabling participants to communicate the most important details of their lives.

Aims   To get participants to be specific about the important events of their lives. To enable participants to communicate something about themselves to the group. To make the group better acquainted with one another.

Directions

1   Participants are invited to identify the five most important chapters of their lives so far, as if they were planning the structure of an autobiography, and write these down as headings. Five such headings might be: childhood, going to school, moving to a new town, leaving home, my first job. Under each heading participants write just the first few words that come to mind about that period of their lives.   *5 min.*

2   Each participant will now try to communicate each stage by creating a frozen image. This could be done solo; or it could be done in small groups, with the 'author' sculpting the others under the five chapter headings.   *5 min.*

3   Every participant is now asked to think of a title for their autobiography – something that would encapsulate their life so far. These could be shared with the whole group, each participant offering a short statement (one sentence) on why they have chosen their specific title.   *10 min.*

   As an extension of this phase, participants could be invited to consider whether the title would be different if it were chosen by one of their parents, or a teacher, or a brother or sister. What title might these people choose, and why?

4   Participants should think of the five details that they consider would be most crucial to an understanding of any of their fellow group members, such as family, education, class, place of birth, employment. They decide on one question under each heading that would gain the information needed. Participants get into pairs, and each asks their partner the specific questions. They should try not to write the answers down but attempt to remember through careful listening. They repeat back afterwards a brief version of what has been heard. Partners confirm that they have it right.   *10 min.*

Exercise 2.9 *Time: 40 min.*

PERSONAL ROAD MAPS

5   Participants could develop this exercise by asking a further round of five questions, this time exploring their partner in greater depth. The area of exploration could be relationships, interests, dislikes, fears, talents, or whatever. Again they should formulate five specific questions, following the same procedure as at stage 4. Extra time would be needed.

Feedback and discussion   How does all this knowledge we have gathered help us to gain an understanding of others? How does the knowledge gained about ourselves help us? Do we see any common elements in our past or background and that of others?   *10 min.*

Notes   Certain aspects of participants' upbringing might be revealed that will need further exploration later in the course. Participants should be told this, and agreement about confidentiality established to make the group a safe environment. In all this work, of course, the group members may control or restrict what they reveal about themselves – this should be clearly communicated to them.

Skills   Identifying important events. Selecting. Careful preparation and questioning. Listening and concentration.

Description   An individual and group exercise in which participants share the important moments of their lives with the group.

Aims   For participants to be specific about the key events and influences in their lives, and to share them with the group.

Directions

1   Each participant needs a large sheet of paper. Participants are asked to design a road map which shows the paths and routes they have taken during their lifetime. They should have a choice of whatever colours they require. They can draw signposts at various points to indicate crossroads, hazards, or whatever.   *10 min.*

2   Participants divide into pairs. Each individual shares their map with their partner, who says what they can gather from the drawing. The drawer can then feed back. They swap over.
                                        10 min.

3   An extension of the exercise could be for one participant to enact their journey for the rest of the group. The floor of the working space now becomes the map surface, and the participant traces their footsteps to show the shape of their journey. They could enlist other members of the group to represent the road signs in tableaux. The group can give feedback about what they learned from the presentation.
                                        15 min.

Feedback and discussion   What common threads do participants see in their own lives and the lives of others? Has tracing the map been personally useful? If so, how? How does what they learned help them in their understanding of others?
                                        5 min.

Notes   As a development of this exercise, much later in the course, participants could put the key characters in their lives into the maps. These could be role-played and key incidents re-enacted. The format of the map can be a useful device for exploring complex emotions and events.

Skills   Ability to visualise. Spatial awareness. Clarity. Interpretation.

FOUR WORDS BUILD

Description   An exercise involving work in pairs, small groups and large groups, designed to promote discussion and the exchange of opinions.

Aims   To identify what the group regards as the most important facets of a specific theme. To try to establish a group consensus about the core concepts of a specific theme. To promote an ethos of participation and regard for others' opinions. To enhance group communication and cohesion.

Directions

1   Choose a specific theme for exploration and formulate a key question. For example, as we are looking at the general theme of communication, you could ask each member of the group to write down the first four words that come to mind in response to the question: 'What are the most important things that are needed for effective communication between individuals or groups?'   *2 min.*

2   Once every member has thought of four words, they find a partner. The partners share their words with each other. The aim of this part of the exercise is to select a new combination of four words, ideally two from each partner's list. No new words are to be added. The partners are to look for what they have in common. If their words and ideas are very different, they should look for a compromise by deciding to give up two words each – they simply decide on two words from their own list. In this way the pair will always emerge with a new combination of four words.   *7 min.*

3   Now the process continues in the same pattern. Each pair joins with another pair, and together they eventually emerge with a new combination of four words – the key words from their two lists.   *5 min.*

4   The groups of four join up to make groups of eight, and the process continues until the whole group has synthesised one list of only four words. If time is limited, the facilitator can call for the surviving words after about three rounds. These can be written up on a board, and everyone can be involved in negotiating to find the key words, or to find ways of combining key concepts.   *5 min.*

Feedback and discussion   Focus on how members felt about having to compromise their ideas. How difficult was it to reach agreements with others? Did this change as the groups increased in number? Do they think that this could provide a useful and positive method for group decision-making? Are they satisfied with the end result?   *6 min.*

Notes   The exercise can be made more interesting by specifying that all words must have the same initial letter. (See the example on page 40, where all words begin with 'c'. This example assumes a group of eight.) This 'building' procedure can be used in difficult situations to find out what people think of, say, their youth club. It can be used to tease out the most important points for an agenda for a meeting. The exercise itself promotes debate.

Skills   Negotiation and compromise. Co-operation and understanding. Creative building on ideas.

Example 2.10

FOUR WORDS BUILD

What does drama mean to you?

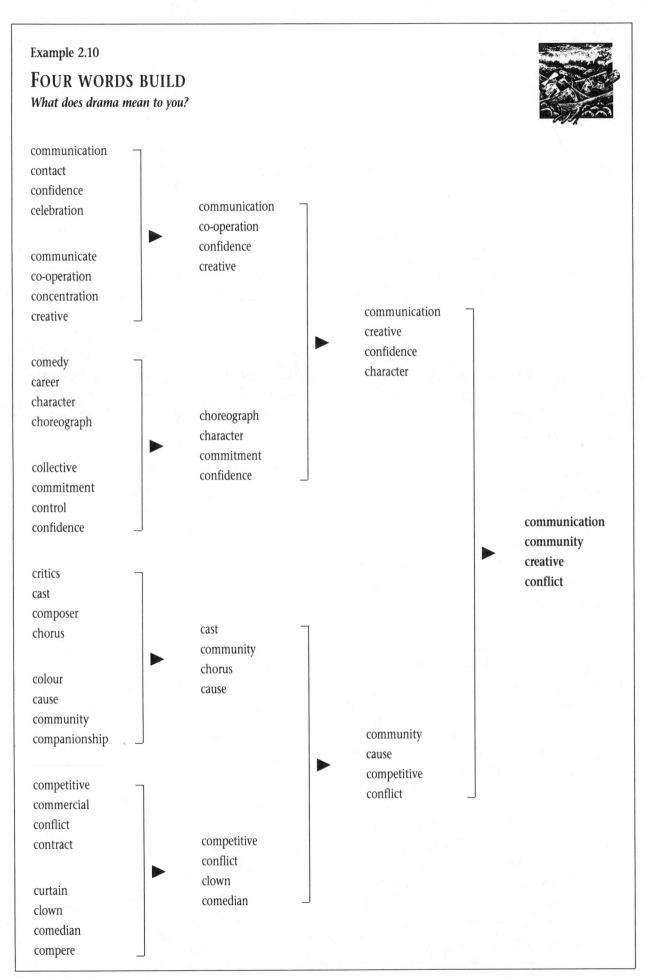

communication
contact
confidence
celebration

communicate
co-operation
concentration
creative

→

communication
co-operation
confidence
creative

→

communication
creative
confidence
character

comedy
career
character
choreograph

collective
commitment
control
confidence

→

choreograph
character
commitment
confidence

→

communication
community
creative
conflict

critics
cast
composer
chorus

colour
cause
community
companionship

→

cast
community
chorus
cause

→

community
cause
competitive
conflict

competitive
commercial
conflict
contract

curtain
clown
comedian
compere

→

competitive
conflict
clown
comedian

Exercise 2.11 *Time: 20 min.*

CREATIVE LISTENING

Description A creative listening exercise in pairs.

Aims To encourage individuals to listen attentively, without judgment and without imposing their own agenda.

Directions

1 Work in pairs. Partners sit directly opposite each other, at a comfortable distance. One of them speaks about an experience where communication between themselves and another person was successful, effective and satisfactory. The other just sits still and listens, refraining from any kind of response, verbal or bodily. (There should be no nodding in approval, for instance.) There is no feedback when the first partner finishes speaking. *3 min.*

2 The two partners now swap roles, and the listener has a turn at speaking. *3 min.*

3 The first speaker now describes an experience in which communication broke down or was unsuccessful and unsatisfactory. Then the partners swap roles again, and the exercise ends when both have spoken twice and listened twice. *6 min.*

Feedback and discussion There are many questions that you might ask participants. Was it easy just to sit and listen? Did you want to participate by asking questions, making comments, passing judgments, agreeing or disagreeing? Did you find it difficult not to think these things while the other person was talking? What did it feel like to be listened to without interruption? Did you want more interaction? Are you used to being listened to in this manner? Are you used to listening in this manner? Did you want feedback afterwards? Were you eager for discussion afterwards? Is this type of listening useful? In what circumstances? What did this exercise tell you about the way you normally listen to others? Do you consider yourself a good listener? *8 min.*

Notes Creative listening means creating the space for someone else to talk and to be simply listened to, without any comment or judgment. The simple willingness to listen is itself an aspect of creative listening.

Skills Listening. Concentration. Expression.

Exercise 2.12 *Time: 20 min.*

BACK-TO-BACK LISTENING

Description An exercise in pairs exploring the effect of body position in creative listening.

Aims To explore creative listening. To see how the physical positions of listener and speaker influence the way they feel while communicating.

Directions

1 The pair sit opposite each other. Each partner speaks for two-and-a-half minutes while the other listens. They might speak, for example, about someone they admire. There is no feedback or comment. *5 min.*

2 In the next round the chairs are arranged so that the speaker faces the back of the listener's head. On this occasion the topic might be something you really like doing. Each partner has a turn at speaking and listening. *5 min.*

3 For the final round the pair sit back-to-back with their heads touching. The topic might be a happy childhood memory. At the end of this round each partner should have spoken and listened three times. *5 min.*

Feedback and discussion Which position felt best for the speaker? Why? Which position felt best for the listener? Why? What difficulties did the participants have in any of the three positions? In everyday life, do they ever feel they are talking to the back of someone's head? Discussion could focus on eye contact, difficulties with concentration, creative listening techniques. As listeners, are participants finding it easier to clear their heads of their own thoughts, prejudices and emotions, and be present for the speaker? *5 min.*

Notes It is possible to combine this exercise with any specific set of questions to explore a theme. You could also explore the effect of distance, getting the pair to move closer together and further apart. Or set both both partners speaking animatedly at the same time, so that neither can hear the other. The main aim of all this work is to get people thinking about the dynamics of communication. It can also help group members get to know each other better.

Skills Listening. Concentration. Expression.

Exercise 2.13 *Time: 25 min.*

TELEPHONE CALL

Description   A role-play exercise in pairs, using an imaginary phone call to explore active listening.

Aims   To explore questions and approaches which enable a speaker to give difficult information. To listen and extract relevant information. To explore active listening.

Directions

1   Participants work in pairs, sitting back-to-back. The caller gets a problem written on a card. This is not revealed to the receiver. Usable problems could be:

* You are 16 and pregnant.
* You are being harassed at work.
* You have discovered that your partner is having a relationship with someone else.
* You want to leave home.
* You are lonely and depressed.   *2 min.*

2   The caller starts talking, but doesn't immediately reveal the problem. They find it difficult to talk about, and need to be encouraged by the receiver. They might begin by talking about the problem indirectly, perhaps by talking about something else.

Slowly, without intimidating the caller, the listener needs to get deeper into the problem, actively responding and acknowledging the feelings of the caller. Once this has been achieved, the listener might find that the caller can come to some decision without being given any advice whatsoever. When a decision is reached, the call ends.   *8 min.*

3   The caller can now give feedback to the listener. The process can be repeated, with the caller becoming the listener.
                                                                   8 min.

Feedback and discussion   What listening techniques worked best? What techniques didn't work? What difficulties did the listeners have? What difficulties did the callers have? How do participants understand the difference between active response and advice-giving? What are the pros and cons of the one and the other? Would it have been easier if they had been face-to-face? Did they find both roles difficult, or was one easier than the other?   *7 min.*

Notes   Active listening involves aspects of creative listening. On this occasion, however, the listener must not only *be* there but must let the caller *know* they are there. Developing the listening into a more active style while helping the caller express themselves openly is difficult. The focus should always be on the listening, and not on the listener's conversation or advice. The listener never takes over, but through careful listening helps the caller to say what they need to say.

Skills   Patience. Sensitivity. Listening (active and creative). Selective and careful questioning. Timing.

Exercise 2.14   *Time: 20 min.*

CIRCLE STORY BUILD

Description   A storytelling exercise in small groups.

Aims   To develop careful listening. To develop sensitivity and teamwork. To develop concentration and memory skills.

Directions

1   Groups of six are ideal for this exercise. The group sits in a small circle. They need a topic to start with. It could be the story of a young person going to a job interview. Once the topic is decided, they should ideally decide the age, sex, and other broad characteristics of the protagonist.   *5 min.*

2   One member of the group begins to tell the story, contributing only about three sentences of narrative. The story is then continued by the person on their left, who also contributes only three sentences or so. And so on, around the circle. Participants should aim to develop incidents and characters without undermining the continuity of the story.

3   The role of the members listening is vital. They need to retain what has gone before, and have some sense of the mood of the story, in order to be able to continue when their turn comes round. The group can decide when the topic is exhausted, or a time limit can be set in advance.   *10 min.*

Feedback and discussion   Did they find it easy? What difficulties were there? Was the mood kept? Did members take care how they handed over to the next member? Did members present their bit of the story clearly and to the whole group? Was there good eye contact? Did members feel it worked? Was there a feeling of achievement when it went well? Was everyone brief? Could people remember all the details? *5 min.*

Notes   This exercise is a good way of building team communication. It is also a useful way of raising and exploring issues. To make the exercise more difficult, members could be restricted to one sentence each, then later to (say) three words or, even more difficult, one word. But for a serious exploration of issues it is better to stick to three sentences each. This gives more scope for development.

Skills   Concentration. Memory. Imagination. Co-operation. Listening. Sensitivity. Timing.

Session 3

Introduction   Communication: concentration and interaction; body language and interpretation; use of language and clarity.   *10 min.*

Reflection   *10 min.*

Notes   Exercise 3.15 is a warm-up listening exercise requiring careful concentration. Exercise 3.16 is a demanding interactive communication exercise. We suggest you do both. Exercise 3.17 is a physical exercise that we recommend as an introduction to the exploration of body language. Choose 3.18 or 3.19, whichever is more suitable for your particular circumstances, as an exercise in body language. Choose 3.20 or 3.21 to explore clarity of expression. Exercise 3.22, which completes the section on fuel, explores differences in our use of language. Session 3 includes six exercises apart from the introduction and reflection.

Exercise 3.15 *Time: 10 min.*

REPEATING THE FACTS

Description An exercise in pairs involving memory and concentration.

Aims To practise listening skills. To practise retelling a story as accurately as possible.

Directions

1 Participants in pairs. One partner tells the other how they got to the session that day – including all the details from leaving home or work or wherever until they entered the door of the workshop venue. (Alternatively, they could recall a recent incident which involved them personally in some kind of conflict.) *90 sec.*

2 When the story is over, the listener retells the story in the second person ('You . . . '). When the retelling is complete, the teller confirms or corrects the facts and comments on omissions. The listener can also comment on the teller's style, and whether this helped or hindered their absorption and recollection of detail. *90 sec.*

3 The partners now swap roles and repeat the exercise. *3 min.*

Feedback and discussion What difficulties did listeners have in remembering information? What could have made it easier? What helped you in the way the story was told? What hindered you in the way the story was told? *4 min.*

Notes A good general communication exercise, focusing on listening skills but also looking at presentation techniques. The communicator is really aware of the fact that there is a listener and works hard to make life easier for them. It could be good to have an observer there to give impartial feedback. Developing good observation and feedback skills is a useful spin-off from this kind of work. The exercise is developed further in Exercise 5.8.

Skills Concentration. Memory. Delivery. Clarity.

Exercise 3.16 *Time: 40 min.*

HIDDEN THOUGHTS

Description A difficult communication exercise in groups of four, using role-play.

Aims To achieve close teamwork and communication. To explore the hidden thoughts behind what we say to each other.

Directions

1 Divide into teams of four. Two characters will be having a conversation, but for the purposes of this exercise two group members will be playing each character. One group member plays the voice of the character; another plays the character's hidden thoughts – the thoughts underlying what is actually being expressed by the voice. Take the groups slowly through an explanation. Demonstrate using four participants attempting to do the exercise. *15 min.*

2 So, in a team of four we have Voice 1 and Thoughts 1, Voice 2 and Thoughts 2. The voices can't speak unless their thoughts have spoken to them. So let's say that Thoughts 1 starts. The situation might be between a parent and child – a son telling his mother that his girlfriend is pregnant, for example. Voice 1 will follow Thoughts 1, but with an opening statement that might not flow directly from the thoughts. For example:

THOUGHTS 1 (SON): My mother's going to be mad. She'll kick me out. I need her help.
VOICE 1 (SON): What you doing this evening, mum? I might watch football. Arsenal's got to win.

Thoughts 2 has to reply before Voice 2 can begin:

THOUGHTS 2 (MOTHER): What the hell has he done to his hair?
VOICE 2 (MOTHER): What do you think I'm doing? What I'm always doing! The dinner, the dishes, the washing . . .

The voices are listening to their own thoughts while at the same time listening to the other voice and having to interpret the situation as well. In the given example, Voice 2 (mother) must accept her thought about her son's haircut, but she can choose either to express that thought directly or to cover it up.

Exercise 3.16 *Continued*

Either way the thought informs her. The conversation follows a set pattern:

The group can pause for consultation if they feel they are not communicating well. They can stop when they think they have a resolution.

3   While the group is getting to grips with the exercise, it is best to build the subject matter slowly by starting with a light situation, progressing to a tricky situation, and then taking on a really difficult and highly charged one, like the one suggested above. Spend four minutes on each of the three role-plays, with a minute's reflection after each one. Participants could now swap roles, but extra time will have to be allocated.

15 min.

Feedback and discussion   The focus of the discussion could be the relationship between what we say and how we actually feel. Why do we have blocks when expressing our feelings? When is it appropriate not to say how we feel? How can we tell when someone is concealing their thoughts? Was it difficult for the voices to interpret the situation and decide what to say?

10 min.

Notes   This exercise is a difficult one, and needs plenty of preparation. Ideally, participants should already have done all the various communication and listening exercises suggested in this section. Later on, the course will focus on specific conflicts and dilemmas within a character: see Exercise 7.5.

It is a good idea to have an observer for this exercise who can give feedback and who could also halt the discussion if they felt that one of the teams would benefit from a quick consultation.

Skills   Concentration. Sensitivity. Judgment. Listening. Improvisation.

Exercise 3.17   *Time: 20 min.*

OPEN AND CLOSED

Description   A physical group exercise exploring the concept of body language.

Aims   To explore 'open' and 'closed' bodily positions and how we use them in everyday interaction. To see how these positions influence communication.

Directions

1   Ask each member of the group to think of an open shape. for one of their hands and a closed shape for the other. These shapes are now shared with the whole group.

2 min.

2   Ask everyone to think of an open gesture and a closed gesture. These are now shared with the group. A short discussion could follow, looking at the main characteristics of these positions. How do people feel when using them? When would they use them?

3 min.

3   Number the members of the group as 1s, 2s and 3s. All the 1s will sit on the floor, all the 2s will sit in chairs, and all the 3s will stand. In those positions they will each adopt an open shape. Share them.

3 min.

4   Then ask everyone to change slowly from the open shape to a closed shape, all at the same time. You could then have the 1s start from the closed position, the 2s from the open, and the 3s from the closed. It is interesting to see the two-way flow of movement from one to the other.

3 min.

5   A further development could be to put people in pairs. They could then respond to each other. A could close off, with B closing off as well in response; then A could open out, with B likewise opening out in response. Alternatively, A and B could respond to each other by adopting contradictory postures, with closure eliciting openness and *vice versa*. Watch the effects.

3 min.

Feedback and discussion   The discussion could look at physical contact as a development of open and closed positions. Do the group see any differences in the style of physical contact between men and between women? Do the men and the women in the group have different views about this?

6 min.

Notes A good exercise for awareness of how we use our bodies and how we read body language in others. An exploration of how body language varies from culture to culture would be valuable.

Skills Physical awareness. Physical expression. Interpretation.

Exercise 3.18 *Time: 25 min.*

BREAKING THE CODE

Description A small-group exercise involving one member of each group in careful observation of the behaviour of the others.

Aims To explore body language. To develop observation skills. To explore the effect of group behaviour on an individual.

Directions

1 Divide the participants into groups of four or five. One person from each group leaves the room. The others think of something physical they will all do when having a discussion (or performing some other agreed activity) in front of the person who is at present outside the room. *3 min.*

2 The outsider re-enters the room and starts a careful observation of the group, who are following the agreed strategy. When the outsider feels they have 'broken the code', they start to use the code themselves and interact with the rest of the group. If they are correct, the group will accept them as one of their own; if they are mistaken, the group will continue to ignore them. The outsider will then have to continue observing until they get the correct code and gain acceptance by the group. *5 min.*

3 Another group member can now have a turn. The group can make the code more difficult and sophisticated every time they repeat the exercise. *10 min.*

Feedback and discussion How did the outsider feel? What did they discover when trying to crack the code? How did the group members feel during the exercise? How does this process relate to what happens in everyday interaction? Do the participants have any observations and comments on body language in general? *7 min.*

Notes This exercise could be used to explore the use of verbal codes in a 'closed' group, to see how a group can develop exclusive uses of language. (An example of a verbal code might be: all sentences spoken have to begin with a word starting with 'w'.) The group could combine a verbal code with a physical code. (An example of a physical code might be: all group members must make eye contact with the appointed group leader before they speak to any other member.)

This exercise could be taken beyond communication to explore other aspects of closed groups. How do gangs operate in terms of language, body language, behaviour, values, fashion, and so on? What is it like to try to gain entry to a closed group? What messages do closed groups give outsiders? Why do people need closed groups?

Skills Careful observation. Teamwork and group planning. Concentration.

Exercise 3.19 *Time: 25 min.*

READING THE FACE

Description A paired exercise involving intense facial observation.

Aims To encourage observation of subtle changes of facial expression and to relate them to emotions.

Directions

1 Participants think of three specific incidents in which they remember feeling exhilarated (such as going downhill fast on a bicycle), sad (such as an old friend moving away), and happy (such as hearing good news). Urge participants to avoid traumatic experiences when recalling something that saddened them. The exercise is not intended to be an ordeal.

3 min.

2 Participants pair off and sit down opposite their partners. Each observes the other, in turn, silently recalling the three experiences. The partner who is doing the recollecting should keep their eyes closed. The observer watches their partner's every facial movement. The facilitator could mention two or three of the following to give participants an idea of what they are looking out for: brows (furrowed, smooth, frowning); eyes (sideways movement); eyelids (fluttering, moving); nostrils (flaring, nose twitching); lips (any movement, curling, twitching, etc.); chin (wobbling); skin (tightening, slackening); breathing (change in pattern).

Speakers should begin each recollection by telling their partner which experience it deals with (exhilarated, happy, or sad), and end by announcing that they have finished. Observers may note down their observations if they wish.

10 min.

3 When each person has had a turn at recollection and observation, each goes back over the three experiences in a different sequence, again silently, while the observer watches to see if they can tell which experience it is.   *5 min.*

Feedback and discussion What observations did you make? What difficulties did you have? What did you find easy? What did you gain from the exercise? We constantly receive subtle messages from the faces of others, and sometimes we are not aware of them, although we may be subconsciously affected.

Likewise, what we are thinking and feeling is reflected in some way in our own facial expressions and gestures. *7 min.*

Notes This is a useful exercise for building intimacy and trust within the group. Careful observation of this kind is an important skill for mediation and conflict resolution work, and can enhance personal effectiveness in meetings. It is useful to be able to listen with eyes as well as ears.

Skills Careful observation. Receiving subtle communication.

Exercise 3.20 *Time: 15 min.*

STICKING TO THE POINT

Description A discussion game in small groups encouraging clear expression.

Aims To encourage clarity of expression, with the emphasis on economy, relevance and continuity.

Directions

1 Participants divide into groups of four. One member is nominated to be the first speaker. They tell the rest of the group what their topic is: for example, *My family*. Another member of the group agrees to act as timekeeper and adjudicator. *10 min.*

2 The speaker talks for one minute on their chosen topic. The other two members will listen closely and call out any of the following 'offences' if they feel the speaker has been 'guilty' them: repetition (unnecessary reiteration of facts or details); digression (anything off the point or irrelevant to the subject matter); hesitation (any lengthy pause in the delivery).

3 If the listeners call out any of these offences, the speaker stops and the timekeeper adjudicates as to whether an offence has indeed been committed. Then the clock is restarted (the timekeeper should ideally have a stopwatch) and the speaker continues until they are stopped again or the minute is up. The timekeeper keeps a record of how many legitimate calls were made during the minute, and what the offences were.

4 Everyone in the group should speak on their own topic, and the role of timekeeper/adjudicator should also rotate.

Feedback and discussion How did speakers feel about their performance? Did they find that they were stopped on one particular offence, or a good spread of the three? Was it easy to spot offences when listening? What skills did the adjudicator need to assess calls and pass an opinion on them? Was the decision of the adjudicator readily accepted? Did the adjudicator listen to disagreements and were they prepared to change their mind? *5 min.*

Notes The game can be played on a competitive basis by keeping scores; or the timekeeper can feed back their notes to the speaker, so that each member can try to improve their performance. The speaker can take a more abstract topic: for example, *My favourite colours and how they affect me*, or *My opinions on current television programmes for lesbian and gay people*. The topics could be factual, personal, political or whatever. This exercise is a good way for members to get to know each other better, as well as a good way of practising clear presentation methods.

Skills   Listening. Concentration. Clarity of thought, expression and presentation. Decision-making.

Exercise 3.21   *Time: 15 min.*

PULL OVER!

Description   An exercise in pairs involving the giving of clear instructions.

Aims   To explore the importance of clarity in the giving of instructions.

Directions

1   In pairs, partner B is to instruct partner A to put on a shoe. Partner A takes one of their shoes off (preferably a shoe with laces – it is more of a challenge). They are to pretend that they have never seen a shoe before and do not even know the names of the different parts (such as heel, sole or laces).

5 min.

2   Partner B begins instructing A. Partner A follows the instructions to the letter. If A gets stuck it is up to B to guide A out of the difficulty. A never talks. When the exercise is completed, the partners swap round.

3   Partner A now instructs partner B to put on a long-sleeved pullover. The same procedure applies.   *5 min.*

Feedback and discussion   Did people find it difficult to give clear instructions? What was it like to be on the receiving end? Did instructors find that they improved as they went along? What frustrations did they encounter? What satisfactions did they experience?   *5 min.*

Notes   Putting on a tie is another difficult task. Further discussion could be on conflict which arises from lack of clarity, and on how the exercise relates to assertiveness. There should have been lots of fun as well as frustration during the exercise.

Skills   Clarity. Practical visualisation. Decision-making.

Exercise 3.22   *Time: 20 min.*

WHAT LANGUAGE DO YOU SPEAK?

Description   An individual and paired exercise looking at the way we use language, and what it can tell us about ourselves.

Aims   To encourage awareness of the language we use, and of its differences from the language of others. To explore ways of communicating with those whose language differs from ours.

Directions

1   Participants are asked to think about a memorable incident from their childhood. In what way do they remember it? The visual or the emotional aspects? Or the smell or the physical feel of it? Participants note down which of these areas they find easiest to conjure up. When they are having difficulty trying to remember something, which part of the memory comes back first?   *5 min.*

2   Individually, participants are invited to think about the language they use in dialogue with the people they are close to. Which of the following phrases would they use more easily: 'I'm out of touch' (tactile); 'I just don't see it' (visual); 'I don't hear your meaning' (aural); 'I can't get hold of it' (physical)? Individually, participants are invited to list familiar phrases under these headings: visual, physical, aural, tactile. They can add any others they think of.   *5 min.*

3   In pairs they share their lists and any thoughts they have had during the exercise. What kind of language do they use? Are their closest friends the ones who use the same language?
                                                      5 min.

Feedback and discussion   Invite participants to think about the people they have difficulty communicating with. Do they speak the same language? If not, how can they adapt in order to get through to them? Apart from spoken language, how do they best receive information – through the written word or through pictures? Or through any other means? How can this exercise help in developing our communication skills?   *5 min.*

Notes   This exercise is useful for bringing up questions about how communication is affected by the differences in our use of language. It could be extended into a study of our personal language histories – that is, how we remember events and

what that tells us about our way of seeing the world. Each of us has a personal language history which relates to our personality and our perceptions as much as to the way we were taught to speak.

Skills   Self-analysis and self-awareness. Recognition of personal communication habits and skills.

THE SPARK

Immediate responses and coping strategies

THE SPARK
Immediate responses and coping strategies

The raw material of fire lies still, but alive. Somewhere a live wire flashes, somewhere lightning strikes, somewhere there is friction. Sparks fly. Some fall on the earth, and die. Some fall on damp wood, and fade. Some fall on dry wood, and live.

THERE are constant tensions, pressures and frustrations in our lives. Sometimes we rise to them and cope; sometimes they spark us off, and distress and tensions grow. Some people are more 'sparky' than others. They are the igniters of the fire, the hot-tempered initiators of conflict. We all react differently to different sparks; we all send different ones flying. Sometimes we are 'sparky', sometimes the opposite. Intervening in the development of the conflict at this stage is a job for the listener within us all. There is more opportunity for successful intervention before the fire really catches hold. Listening is a first step.

Focus   Sparks as the incidents, situations, reactions that ignite the fuel: combustibility, our ways of responding to conflict; self-awareness in group situations; self-presentation, the use of the voice and body.

Aims   To examine our responses when the sparks begin to fly: to determine how combustible we are; to be aware of how combustible those around us are; understanding the nature of points of friction; putting our own physical resources into practice; exploring our present strategies for dealing with conflict and exploring new ways of responding.

Key concepts   Personal combustibility; combustible situations; group dynamics; presentation – energy; sparking points – friction; interaction – tension; responding – reacting.

Key questions   How combustible are you? How combustible are those around you? How easily are sparks noticed? How do we respond to sparks or situations of tension? What is your most common role in group situations? How does this role change according to circumstances? To what extent do you use your personal resources of voice, body, energy? To what extent can the use of these resources influence situations of conflict?

This section contains three two-and-a-half-hour sessions. Session 4 deals with combustibility, immediate responses, and changing reactions into responses. Session 5 deals with self-presentation, and how the use of the voice and body can influence situations. Session 6 focuses on self-awareness, group dynamics, self-presentation in a group situation, and how our roles change with circumstances.

All training techniques (such as brainstorm, role-play and tableau work) are explained in TRAINING FOR TRAINERS.

Session 4

Introduction Personal and situational points of conflict: combustibility (what sparks you off); immediate responses (thinking on your feet); changing reactions into responses.

10 min.

4.1	RED FLAGS	*35 min.*
4.2	IMMEDIATE RESPONSES	*50 min.*
4.3	THREE TO ONE	*45 min.*

Reflection *10 min.*

Notes This session includes three longer exercises. Exercise 4.1 focuses on situations that provoke our anger; Exercise 4.2 gives an opportunity to practise responses to difficult situations; and Exercise 4.3 gives an opportunity to plan and rehearse strategic responses to situations that are not easy to handle.

Exercise 4.1 *Time: 35 min.*

RED FLAGS

Description An exercise involving thinking about our emotions and sharing them in pairs and small groups.

Aims To explore language and situations to which we have strong reactions, and to work on future responses to them.

Directions

1 Give each participant a copy of Handout 4.1A, RED FLAGS (page 55), and ask them to fill it in. *5 min.*

2 In pairs, ask the participants to share as much or as little of their lists as they want to. Then ask them to find one emotion from each sheet to enact together. If one partner has said that they switch off when someone uses long, elaborate words, one partner will take on the role of speaking multisyllabically and the other will enact the switching-off reaction. *10 min.*

3 In small groups, the pairs show their examples and ask the others to guess which 'red flag' each scene relates to. *10 min.*

Feedback and discussion What does this exercise teach you about yourself? How could anticipating your emotional reactions help? What advantages are there in seeing what the 'red flags' of others are? *10 min.*

Notes How we react in different situations is a function of who we are and how we feel others perceive us. Looking at labels is a useful way of exploring this. If you have time, the group could fill out Handout 4.1B, RED LABELS (page 56), focusing on labels that they are given by others. What are the labels you carry? How do they determine your responses – for example, as a pensioner, feminist, black person, immigrant, refugee, socialist, disabled person, taxpayer, religious person, someone with HIV, a business person?

Some situations will always make us angry – to witness racist abuse in the street, for example. Sometimes we *allow* situations or people to make us angry – when someone crosses lanes without indicating, perhaps. But we are always responsible for the ways we react to situations that 'make' us angry, whether the anger is sparked off by deep-rooted conviction or just a bad mood.

Skills Self-awareness. Role-play. Creative thinking.

RED FLAGS

What people/things/situations make me angry?

What things/people/situations frighten or upset me?

What sorts of behaviour/gestures/words make me switch off?

What situations/things/people irritate me?

What makes me uneasy?

What people/things/situations make me frustrated?

RED LABELS

As a .... *(any label you have that others give you, or that you give yourself)*

| What's good about being a ... ? | What's difficult about being a ... ? |

| What makes me angry? | What frightens me? |

| What frustrates me? | What makes me switch off? |

Exercise 4.2   *Time: 50 min.*

IMMEDIATE RESPONSES

Description   An interactive game in pairs using prepared cards and improvised responses, leading to work on difficult personal situations.

Aims   To find effective responses to difficult situations. To explore ways of raising our status after a put-down. To find a good response to a situation we are likely to come up against.

Directions

1   Participants divide into small groups. This is a game in which everyone has a turn at being both the provoker (A) and the respondent (B), and at acting as an arbiter. Give out to each group a pile of the STRATEGY CARDS: PHASE 1 (pages 58–59), on which are written various lines for A to say. A picks up the top card. B moves over to face A. A approaches B with the line on their card. As B had no idea what the card said they give their immediate response, with the aim of raising their bruised status. The remainder of the group act as arbiters and decide whether B's response was effective. If the arbiters consider that it was, the card is discarded; if not, the card returns to the pile for someone else to have a go at.

   A and B return to their seats and the next two people take their places. Continue in this way either until all the cards have been used or until a predetermined time limit has been reached.   *15 min.*

2   In the same groups, everyone is given a card on which is written a type of provocation – see STRATEGY CARDS: PHASE 2 (page 60). Individually everyone decides on a line appropriate to the brief, without telling anyone else what it is. The game goes on in the same way as before, but this time the provoker tells the respondent what their original brief was.

   15 min.

3   Participants divide into pairs. Ask each person to think of a provocative situation they face or are likely to be faced with soon. This is a chance for them to try out different responses with their partners.   *10 min.*

4   Participants now share some of the successful responses from stage 3.   *5 min.*

Feedback and discussion   How did people raise their status? What was an assertive response? How do they tend to react to provocative situations? How would they like to respond?
   5 min.

Notes   The second half of the exercise is an opportunity to rehearse strategies to deal with a difficult situation. It is important that individual needs are recognised and valued. A solution or strategy will not necessarily suit everyone. What matters is that each individual is happy with their own particular solution. It would be a good idea to hear from the group about experiences and feelings they have had when on the receiving end of offensive remarks or comments. It is important to assist anyone who is upset by the work done in this exercise.

Skills   Quick responses. Creative thinking. Assertiveness. Creating strategies and problem-solving.

STRATEGY CARDS: PHASE 1

SHOP SECURITY STAFF

I saw you – you're the one that did it!

THE SPARK
4.2A

TICKET COLLECTOR

What do you mean, you can't find your ticket?

THE SPARK
4.2A

PARENT

What are you doing outside my daughter's bedroom at three in the morning?

THE SPARK
4.2A

IN A QUEUE

Excuse me, I was first!

THE SPARK
4.2A

IN A PUB

Sorry, but we can't allow children in here.

THE SPARK
4.2A

FRIENDS

You've kept me waiting for three whole hours.

THE SPARK
4.2A

STRATEGY CARDS: PHASE 1

PARENT

It's two a.m. and I told you to be in by eleven!

THE SPARK
4.2A

IN A QUEUE

The queue starts up there, duckie!

THE SPARK
4.2A

IN A PUB

You look lonely – do you mind if I join you?

THE SPARK
4.2A

SOCIAL SETTING

Haven't I seen you somewhere before?

THE SPARK
4.2A

SOCIAL SETTING

Cheer up, love – things could be worse.

THE SPARK
4.2A

CUSTOMS OFFICIAL

One bottle of spirits is the limit.

THE SPARK
4.2A

STRATEGY CARDS: PHASE 2

RACIST COMMENT

THE SPARK
4.2B

SEXIST COMMENT

THE SPARK
4.2B

DECLARATION OF LOVE

THE SPARK
4.2B

GETTING THE SACK

THE SPARK
4.2B

ACCUSATION OF SHOPLIFTING

THE SPARK
4.2B

ANTI-GAY COMMENT

THE SPARK
4.2B

Exercise 4.3 *Time: 45 min.*

THREE TO ONE

Description Interactive work in small groups looking at difficult situations.

Aims To explore different responses to difficult situations. To recognise our current tactics and skills in handling such situations and to learn from the tactics and skills of others. To find appropriate responses to situations we are concerned with. To anticipate difficulties and prepare responses.

Directions

1 Ask participants to think of or write down an incident or situation they recently faced, at work, at home or socially, which they feel they didn't deal with effectively. *5 min.*

2 Participants divide into small groups, and each group agrees on one person's situation to work on. They explore what the following could be in relation to this situation: the most likely response; the most provocative response; and the 'successful' response (that is, the response which works for that person at that time – not necessarily a universally successful approach). The groups role-play the three options. If the most likely corresponds with the most provocative response, there will only be two options to enact. *25 min.*

3 Either join up as a whole group and see some of the options role-played, or join groups together in twos to show their options to each other. *10 min.*

Feedback and discussion What differences were made by the different approaches? What worked and why? In what ways was it familiar or unfamiliar? How often is the likely response the provocative one or the successful one? What skills or tactics are we already using to avoid the provocative response? *5 min.*

Notes The most likely response will often be a response which does not work. If the group feel, in their example, that the most likely response is the successful response, the facilitator could explore the factors which contribute to making the most likely response successful.

Skills Clear thinking. Creative ideas. Improvisation. Finding strong points in ourselves and others.

Session 5

Introduction Self-presentation: making maximum use of our physical resources, and exploring how the use of the voice and body can influence situations. *10 min.*

5.4	SLOW MOTION	*15 min.*
5.5	STATES OF TENSION	*35 min.*
5.6	FIND YOUR VOICE	*20 min.*
5.7	VOICE AND ENERGY FOR CHANGE	*30 min.*
5.8	SLANTED STORYTELLING	*30 min.*

Reflection *10 min.*

Notes Exercises 5.4 and 5.5 are physical exercises promoting greater awareness of energy and balance. Exercise 5.6 explores and promotes the use of the voice in different ways. Exercise 5.7 gives participants the chance to put into practice what they have learned from the above exercises. Exercise 5.8 is a fun exercise to end the session. It explores the ways in which we can distort or misrepresent information that we are communicating to others.

Exercise 5.4   *Time: 15 min.*

SLOW MOTION

Description   An exercise involving individual, pair, and whole-group physical work.

Aims   To develop physical control and balance. To develop concentration.

Directions

1   Ask everyone to stand in a circle with feet slightly apart and parallel, with equal weight on both feet – a comfortable, poised position. Ask them slowly to take the weight off one foot and transfer it to the other; then ask them to reverse this process. As observer you should hardly notice any movement.

2 min.

2   Ask participants to walk from their position in the large circle towards the centre of the circle, again transferring weight from one foot to the other while this time moving very slowly forward. They should stop only when they have reached the centre of the circle, or when their path is blocked by another participant.

3 min.

3   Everyone now walks normally round the room. On *freeze*, everyone stops where they are. Are they standing in a strong, well-balanced position, knees slightly bent, weight evenly distributed, body – although still – not tense and stiff? Try pushing participants gently – from the front, side or behind – and see if they lose their balance. Partners can also do this in pairs, trying all the time to find the strongest and most stable position.

2 min.

4   Participants in pairs, standing opposite each other about six feet apart. Ask partners to move towards each other in slow motion, lifting their arms and moving to a position where they can shake hands. Again the movements should be as slow and as smooth as possible. There should be no talking in the room other than your occasional comments. If one pair finishes early they should silently watch the others.

3 min.

5   Participants remain in pairs. Again in slow motion, one partner attempts to punch the other, who moves to defend themselves. No contact need take place. Like the handshake, this exercise relies on good balance and evenly distributed weight.

2 min.

6   You could end with a larger-group or whole-group slow-motion scene – a group fight or dancing at the disco, perhaps. You might need extra time for this.

Feedback and discussion   How important is it to have a feeling of control and balance in difficult situations? Did the work give any participants a feeling of confidence? What did it feel like moving slowly? What have they gained from the exercise?

3 min.

Notes   Practice in slow-motion work and freezing can be very useful later on when participants role-play potentially violent situations. Individual participants will need to exercise control and have confidence that others will do the same.

This exercise is also a physical introduction to the idea of balance – being non-defensive (that is, not going backwards) and non-aggressive (that is, not going forwards). It is very useful for achieving focus and control within a hyperactive group. Use the feedback questions throughout the exercise, not just at the end – participants may well need ongoing comments and encouragement.

Skills   Balance. Co-ordination. Teamwork. Concentration.

Exercise 5.5 *Time: 35 min.*

STATES OF TENSION

Description   Individual, pair and group work exploring how situations are influenced by personal energy levels.

Aims   To explore the range of energy levels any individual can utilise, and how these levels can change the way people respond to us. To look at ways of using the energy we have, and exploring levels that we find difficult to reach.

Directions

1   Introduce the purpose of this exercise and describe the six different levels of tension:

a   SLOTH/COLLAPSE A state of no energy, just about awake but unable to move or speak clearly.

b   LAID BACK/VERY COOL Using the least energy possible for the situation: slow speech and movement.

c   EVERYDAY/ONE OF THE CROWD A 'normal' energy level: you wouldn't be noticed walking down the street – nothing unusual about you at all.

d   BUSINESSLIKE/ORGANISED Slightly unrelaxed, slight tension: going about a task that needs to be completed.

e   WORRY/TENSION Unrelaxed and tense, slight panic creeping in: things are not going according to plan.

f   PANIC/HYPERACTIVITY Growing into real panic – pulling out all the stops.   *5 min.*

2   Ask each participant to explore for themselves what their idea of each level is. Using all the space, get the group to stand up and give them a specific task such as walking to the station to catch a train. Start from level *a* and remind them of each level as you slowly take them through to *f*.   *10 min.*

3   In groups of six or as the whole group, depending on confidence levels, ask two volunteers to role-play to the rest. The group decides what level of tension each character is at and gives them a situation in which to interact, such as standing in a queue hoping to get tickets. During the role-play, the group can freeze the actors and change the tension levels, then unfreeze them and observe what effect the change has.   *5 min.*

4   In groups of six, the participants are given a line on a card – for example, 'What do you think you are doing?' In turn they enter the space and say the line, each using a different energy level.   *10 min.*

Feedback and discussion   What moods came across in stage four, using the same line six times? What effect could energy levels have on specific situations? When are certain levels more appropriate than others?   *5 min.*

Notes   Try to find out which levels people found easiest to use, and why they found certain levels difficult to reach or uncomfortable to use. Different people will have different ideas about each energy level and what it means to them. There are no rights or wrongs. The exercise is developed further in Exercise 5.7.

Skills   Improvisation. Role-play. Control. Inventiveness. Concentration.

FIND YOUR VOICE

Description An individual and pair exercise exploring tone of voice.

Aims To explore the range of vocal tone that any individual can utilise. To see how the use of the voice can affect how others respond to us, and how we feel in various situations.

Directions

1 Participants in a circle. Each in turn says 'O Henry!' in a different way. (There are meant to be at least a hundred ways of saying it.)   *2 min.*

2 Give each participant a card with a simple phrase written on each side. These will be short statements, commands and questions like 'I don't agree', 'Who is it?', 'Meet me later', 'What have you lost?' Each participant chooses one of the phrases from their card. All walk round the room exploring these phrases in four different ways: certain/confident, loudly and softly; then uncertain/unconfident, loudly and softly. Participants are likely to find that uncertain and loudly, and certain and softly are harder than their more common counterparts. Working in pairs, participants help support and coach each other.   *3 min.*

3 In pairs the group turn their cards over and start experimenting with that phrase. This time they will be trying out different moods and emotions, again with both their soft and their loud voices. Different ways of saying could include:
LOUDLY: Assertive, aggressive, scared, commanding, excited.
SOFTLY: Gentle, firm, scared, ashamed, supportive.   *5 min.*

4 Ask one partner in each pair to nominate a mood, tone and volume, and the other to try their phrase in that way. They then swap over.   *5 min.*

Feedback and discussion What observations did participants make about the ways in which the sense of the phrase changed? What did participants find difficult? In what ways would they like to develop their voices further?   *5 min.*

Notes A good exercise for assertiveness work. The more relaxed and warmed-up the group are, the better.

Skills Concentration. Control. Imagination. Listening.

VOICE AND ENERGY FOR CHANGE

Description A small-group exercise to put into practice the work started in Exercises 5.5 and 5.6.

Aims To consolidate previous work on voice and energy levels. To use both voice and energy together. To implement change within a role-play by adapting voice and energy.

Directions

1 Put the participants into groups of three or four and give out the phrase cards used in the last exercise. Each group has to find a way of combining their phrases to make a short scene that makes sense. They will need to decide who they are, where they are, and what is happening. Ask them to think about how they are going to say their specific lines and what the energy level of their character is.   *10 min.*

2 The group should run through their scene. Now put two groups together so that they can share their work. The observer group should give feedback on whether the other group's scene was clear and audible, and what they understood was being communicated. Then suggestions can be made as to which characters might make a change either to their use of voice or to their energy level. The scene can then be replayed incorporating these suggestions. The observer group can assess how a change in one character affects the other characters – did they change too? How? The active group now becomes the observer group.   *15 min.*

Feedback and discussion Share the observations that were made in the different groups. How was change effected? How did it feel to make the changes? Did changes to a character mean that they progressed better or worse in the rerun? Did the changes to one character force the others to adapt? Did these changes take the others by surprise? Maybe you broke a regular pattern of behaviour? How is this exercise relevant to real situations?   *5 min.*

Notes This exercise can open up a whole new range of possibilities for members of the group. It is the beginning of an exploration of how many choices we do actually have. It is also a non-threatening look at making personal changes and examining personal habits. Later you could be exploring more sensitive or personal subjects and material, like violent and aggressive behaviour and change, and these exercises will help to prepare for this by building confidence in and awareness of effective communication.

Skills Role-play. Imagination. Decision-making. Teamwork. Concentration.

Exercise 5.8 *Time: 30 min.*

SLANTED STORYTELLING

Description A storytelling exercise exploring bias.

Aims To explore how prejudice can slant the way a story is told or how facts are communicated.

Directions

1 In pairs, follow the same procedure as outlined in steps 1 to 2 of Exercise 3.15.   *3 min.*

2 Now give everyone an attitude or a mood or a situation written down on a card. Ask them not to disclose what is on their card. They now have to work out how to retell the story using that interpretation. Examples of these cards could be:

- It is the funniest story you have ever told or heard.
- You are a department head in the secret service and are telling the story of a suspect's movements.
- You are dying to go to the toilet, but must first finish telling the story.
- You detest the person you are talking about.
- You are lying about your movements.
- You are stirring things up with some gossip.
- It is the saddest story you have ever told or heard. *10 min.*

3 Individuals now present their stories to the rest of the group, who try to guess what was on the card. Once the tellers have revealed what the statement was, the listeners might suggest how they could have been more effective.   *12 min.*

Feedback and discussion In what ways was information changed and reshaped according to the presenter's bias? Is this a process that is easy to detect in real life? Do we always change the information we pass on? In what ways and in what situations have we done this?   *5 min.*

Notes Cards could cover specific issues rather than moods. Participants might, for example, be invited to tell the story from a racist point of view. With cards such as the ones suggested above, however, this exercise should be very entertaining and a lot of fun. The exercise involves skills and techniques covered in this session as a whole.

Skills Interpretation. Improvisation. Presentation. Observation.

Session 6

Introduction Self-awareness; group dynamics; self-presentation in a group; how our roles change according to circumstances.   *10 min.*

Notes Exercises 6.9 and 6.10 both look at group dynamics and at how individuals are functioning within the group. Exercise 6.11 gives participants a chance to assess and reflect on what they have learnt in the previous exercises. If this reflection is felt to be unsuitable or unnecessary, then the extra time could be allocated to exercises 6.12 and 6.13, making them each 40 minutes rather than 30 minutes. Exercise 6.12 gives group members a chance to present a piece of their own to the group (preparation for this will have to be done in advance). Exercise 6.13 explores group communication. It can be used to air and discuss difficult topics or feelings in a safe environment.

Exercise 6.9   *Time: 30 min.*

BUILDING A TOWER

Description A large-group practical exercise on group dynamics and observation.

Aims To create a greater self-awareness in the group. To explore the different ways in which individuals work in a group environment. To develop observation and feedback skills.

Directions

1 Participants divide into two groups. One group becomes the builders, and the other group the observers. The builders receive a pile of newspapers and a few rolls of masking tape. Their task is to build a tower out of the paper which must be freestanding with three points touching the floor. It must be at least six feet high.   *3 min.*

2 Give the group a maximum of 12 minutes to complete the task. Instruct the observers to look at the group dynamics as well as the process involved.   *12 min.*

3 On completion, the observers give their feedback. Also allow time for the builders to make comments and give their observations. One way of structuring the observation process is to give each observer one builder to make notes on. What was that individual's role in the group? What was their style of work? How did they interact with the others? Does the observer see them as a planner, a doer, a follower, an individualist, an observer, an improviser, etc.?

At the end of the exercise you could ask each builder to give a self-assessment using the same framework. The observers could, in the meantime, do an overall evaluation of how the builders achieved their task. Did they consult? Did they plan? Was there a leader? Was everyone involved? Each builder could then team up with their observer and compare notes.   *10 min.*

Feedback and discussion What does this exercise tell us about teamwork? How do projects run? How do creative tasks get done? What difficulties do groups have in functioning? What difficulties did participants experience during the process?   *5 min.*

Exercise 6.9 *Continued*

Notes   This works both as an exercise in group decision-making and co-operation, and as a study of how creative ideas are taken up or rejected by a group. If you can allocate extra time you could repeat this exercise, builders becoming observers, focusing first on process, then on group dynamics.

Skills   Teamwork. Observation. Feedback. Self- and group-awareness.

Exercise 6.10   *Time: 20 min.*

TESTING THE WATER

Description   An individual exercise in personal reflection.

Aims   To encourage participants to reflect on their own most common patterns of behaviour. To look at how our behaviour varies according to changes in circumstances.

Directions

1   Ask this question: If you are at the seaside, which is the most likely way for you to get into the water? Would you:
- Just run towards the sea and dive in?
- Walk in slowly, wetting your body bit-by-bit and getting used to the temperature?
- Dip your toe in the water, then decide if you'll go in?
- Stand on the beach contemplating the view and surroundings, and considering what you will do next?

5 min.

2   Once everyone in the group has chosen at least one of these, give each type of response a title such as 'plunger', 'wader', 'tester', 'procrastinator'. Discuss the attributes of each of these types of behaviour.   *5 min.*

3   Now ask each participant to consider whether the mode of behaviour they chose is their most common way of behaving. If they find that they behave differently in different circumstances, get them to describe a particular situation and a response. Once they have thought about this, they could share their thoughts in groups of three or so.   *5 min.*

Feedback and discussion   In what ways does our behaviour change in different circumstances? What sort of conflicts could arise when a 'plunger' has to work alongside a 'tester'? In what ways could the two actually benefit one another? What are the positive aspects of each approach? For what reasons do people adopt these different approaches?   *5 min.*

Notes   The assumption here is that a greater awareness of how we respond in different situations increases our understanding of the dynamics involved in conflict situations. It also encourages attention to the behaviour of others, and an understanding of the needs underlying their behaviour.

Skills   Self-awareness. Awareness of types of behaviour.

Exercise 6.11 *Time: 20 min.*

ME IN ACTION

Description A quick exercise to consolidate the work done in Exercises 6.9 and 6.10.

Aims To assess our own most common ways of presenting ourselves. To determine whether these styles of self-presentation are self-imposed or imposed by others. To assess whether we feel liberated or restricted by our self-presentation.

Directions

1 Referring to the two previous exercises, ask participants what they feel are their most common ways of presenting themselves or operating within a group situation. Write up a list of questions for participants to consider: Why do you think you behave in this way? Is there pressure on you to behave like that? What are the payoffs for you – what do you get from that behaviour? Can you imagine using another approach? Would it be very difficult to change? What expectations do you think people (friends, family, acquaintances, your 'enemies') have of you? Would you like to experiment with other behaviours and roles? Ask participants to write down their responses to these questions. *5 min.*

2 In pairs, ask participants to share what they have written down. They can help each other to formulate clear, straightforward replies. *5 min.*

3 In one large group, ask participants to share their responses and look for comparisons and similarities. Every individual should end up with a clear personal goal: for example, 'I would like to try letting others take the initiative in a task or exercise, and try to take a less commanding role.' *5 min.*

Feedback and discussion Do participants feel clearer about their roles, and have they an idea of what they are working towards? What strategy do they need in order to set about achieving their aims? *5 min.*

Notes It is good for participants to say out loud in front of the group what they are trying to change. This means that members can support each other in achieving goals.

Skills Personal reflection. Clarity of thought about self and others. Setting personal goals. Personal observation.

Exercise 6.12 *Time: 30 min.*

SHARING INFORMATION

Description An individual exercise involving the preparation and presentation of information.

Aims To practise good presentation and feedback skills.

Directions

1 Divide into groups of three. Each participant will have previously decided on a subject and prepared for a five-minute presentation. The presentations should deal with practical subjects: for example, how to get good use out of something, how to organise a trip abroad, what to do when buying a second-hand car. Preparation will have involved thinking about structure and timing, and the talk should have been rehearsed before it is presented. Individuals could team up with a partner to give them initial feedback before presenting it to their whole group. Presenters should be conscious of the need to allow space for their listeners to participate. In the groups, each participant takes their turn and gives their presentation. *15 min.*

2 Listeners should be asked to give feedback on each talk. For this purpose, they should each have a copy of Handout 6.12, the PRESENTATION SKILLS CHECKLIST (page 69). Allow three minutes' feedback for each talk. *10 min.*

Feedback and discussion What have the participants gained from delivering their presentation? What have they gained from having to give constructive criticism to others, and to take criticism themselves? What have they learnt from other people's presentations? In what ways were they helped or supported by the personal feedback? *5 min.*

Notes This exercise can be video-recorded so that the participants can criticise themselves as well. The exercise is a good way of sharing and increasing knowledge, as well as encouraging confidence, with an important focus on careful preparation. It builds on earlier exercises looking at voice, body language and energy, and group co-operation and dynamics.

Skills General presentation skills. Giving and taking criticism. Participation. Discussion. Debate. Listening and sharing ideas.

Handout 6.12

PRESENTATION SKILLS CHECKLIST

THERE are many things we need to pay attention to when presenting ourselves, one-to-one, in front of small groups, or in a large group or meeting. Think about how these points relate to your own presentation, and use them as a checklist to assess the effectiveness of others in order to give them feedback. Note that the specifics in this list will vary from situation to situation. For example, the use of eye contact, volume, pace and tone of voice could depend on size of space, age of group, and the culture of the speaker and audience.

FACILITATION AND INTERACTION

- Observation – noticing the group's interest; noticing who wants to speak; assessing group dynamics.
- System for participation – order of speaking; style of feedback; questions to yourself and to other members of the group; time allocated for interaction.
- Getting their attention – appropriate strategies; negotiation of the time, activity or subject; suitable environment created; self-respect, confidence, respect for them.
- Responding to involvement – listening to views expressed; leading and encouraging discussion; seeing that everyone is heard; monitoring group dynamics.

LANGUAGE

- Economical – not too wordy?
- Accessible – simple vocabulary without jargon?
- Clear – well ordered, structured, and summed up?
- Understandable – did the audience understand what was said?

STYLE

- Eye contact – too much/too little?
- Facial expression – expressive, relaxed?
- Gesture and body language – open posture, use of hands, body position relaxed?
- Energy level – too high/too low/ appropriate?
- Pace – too fast/slow, too regular/ irregular?
- Vocal projection – too loud/too soft/appropriate/balanced?
- Tone of voice – too aggressive/ too gentle/well balanced?

Exercise 6.13   *Time: 30 min.*

IN SOMEONE ELSE'S SHOES

Description   A group exercise involving interpretation, sharing and discussion of feelings and opinions held by participants.

Aims   To create empathy and understanding within the group. To create an atmosphere in which group members can share feelings and opinions they might not otherwise feel able to. To practise clear communication of thoughts to others.

Directions

1   Ask participants to write down two statements, one on each side of a small index card, in response to two related questions: for example, *In what way do you feel appreciated and valued by the group?* and *In what way do you feel unappreciated and undervalued by the group?* The statements could also be in response to a specific theme, such as self-image, or something you feel is good or not too good about yourself.   *5 min.*

2   If the subject matter is sensitive, and the participants know each other well enough to recognise each other's handwriting, you could take the statements away and type them up during a break.

3   Redistribute the cards amongst the group, each member having a card written by someone else. In pairs, the partners read their cards to one another, interpreting them as if they were their own, so as to gain an understanding of points of view that they themselves might not share.   *10 min.*

4   Participants get back into a circle. Ask each to read out what was on their card as if it were their own and give a short explanation of it. At this stage there is no comment by the group.   *10 min.*

Feedback and discussion   How has the sharing of this information changed participants' understanding? Did they find it difficult to get into someone else's shoes and understand their point of view? What did it feel like to hear someone else taking on and commenting on their point of view?   *5 min.*

Notes   This exercise can be developed further by exploring the information that has been shared: both the original

statements and the explanations given in stage 4 as to why someone had written it. The exercise has been used successfully for a variety of purposes:

- to create group trust and understanding
- to help towards resolving group disputes
- to assist in the gathering of sensitive information in an unthreatening way
- to help in the resolution of a conflict between two groups, such as management and staff

It can also be interesting to use the exercise for personal problem-solving. Each participant writes a personal difficulty down. Cards are redistributed as before. The focus of the exercise now becomes a sharing of how other members would deal with the problem. In this way the participant who wrote the card can hear a variety of responses from the group and possibly select useful ideas for themselves. Again this is a way of expressing difficulties and sensitive issues in a non-threatening environment.

In awkward situations, the feedback could be structured by using the whip round or the bracelet, whichever is more appropriate (see page 25; see also Exercise 11.9).

Skills   Active listening and interpretation. Creative listening. Concentration. Clarity of expression.

SMOULDERING

Powerlessness and assertiveness

SMOULDERING
Powerlessness and assertiveness

Sparks fly and land. A few catch. There is an indication of fire – slowly smoke begins to rise. The smell of smoke grows as the fuel begins to smoulder. The fuel is burning, but without strength. The smouldering coals lie still, ready either to ignite or to die down.

THERE is trouble brewing now. There is a rumbling of discontent, and the situation is being aggravated by persistent needling. The agitators enjoy themselves. They are rustling the coals to encourage the spark to catch. It is still possible to stamp out the fire at this stage if we recognise that it is there. Being assertive when feeling put down or oppressed, or when unfair demands are being made of you, is one way to prevent escalation of the conflict. When we rumble inside, or feel agitated and refuse to confront the causes, we are refusing to admit to the warning signs of fire – we are allowing ourselves to smoulder.

Focus Short-term and long-term smouldering: differences between personal and positional power; confronting and using power as a positive force; assertiveness as a way of responding to difficult situations.

Aims To understand assertiveness and to implement it in our everyday lives. To recognise the ways we use our power and the ways we experience the power of others. To identify sources of power. To recognising smouldering in the family, at work, in the community, and practise appropriate responses.

Key concepts Power – positional and personal; assertiveness – alternatives to 'attacking' and 'avoiding'; smouldering behaviour; aggression; powerlessness; affirmation.

Key questions How would you recognise smouldering behaviour? How do you smoulder? What are the differences between short-term and long-term smouldering? What is assertive behaviour? In what ways do you experience your own power and the power of others?

This section contains three two-and-a-half-hour sessions. Session 7 deals with feelings of power and powerlessness, and losing and gaining personal power – identifying positive and negative influences on our behaviour. Session 8 looks at assertiveness – expressing feelings and exploring positive responses, and acknowledging and addressing personal needs and group commitments. Session 9 focuses on assertiveness in action, locating smouldering situations and working for appropriate responses.

All training techniques (such as brainstorm, role-play and tableau work) are explained in TRAINING FOR TRAINERS.

Session 7

Exercise 7.1   *Time: 10 min.*

BRAINSTORM

Introduction   Feelings of power and powerlessness; losing and gaining personal power.   *10 min.*

Notes   Exercise 7.1 is an introductory exploration of smouldering behaviour. Exercise 7.2 is a discussion and communication exercise concentrating on the theme of power and powerlessness and sharing personal reflections. Exercise 7.3 is a physical exercise using tableaux to portray situations of power and powerlessness. Exercise 7.4 extends the physical work and explores the ways in which members can present themselves in a confident manner. Exercise 7.5 uses improvisation to explore situations in which we struggle with doubts and lack of confidence.

Description   A verbal exercise for gathering ideas from the group without discussion.

Aims   To bring out the range of opinions and perceptions in the group without discussion or argument. To establish a starting point for the session.

Directions

1   Set a time limit on the exercise (we suggest four minutes) and nominate a timekeeper and a scribe. The scribe will need a large sheet of paper and a marker pen. Introduce the subject, *smouldering*. Explain that the scribe will write down everything that is said during the agreed time. The exercise is an opportunity for people to say whatever they think of in relation to that word. There will be no questioning and no discussion within the time limit, even to ask someone for clarification of what they mean. The only reason for any questions should be if the scribe needs to check whether they have heard a word correctly.

Stress that brainstorming is not about giving explanations for your understanding of the subject. It is instead an opportunity to let your mind rove over the area, finding words that you connect with the subject matter and which may express your understanding of it.

2   During the allowed time, the scribe writes down everything that is said without question or comment.   *4 min.*

Feedback and discussion   Are both positive and negative aspects of the area covered? What are the recurring themes? Are there any words you can link up? What does all this tell you about the group's understanding of *smouldering*?   *6 min.*

Notes   This is a good technique for gathering ideas.

Skills   Quick thinking. Free association. Imagination. Concentration. Group acceptance of ideas.

Exercise 7.2   *Time: 30 min.*

Sharing power

Description   A paired creative listening exercise exploring the theme of power.

Aims   To broaden our understanding of power. To offer a forum in which participants can explore experiences of their own power and that of others. To practise creative listening.

Directions

1   Arrange the seating so that there are two concentric circles of chairs, one circle facing outwards, the other around them and facing inwards. There are an equal number of chairs in the inner and the outer ring. Participants can now arrange themselves on the chairs. Everyone should be facing a partner. Introduce the exercise as a creative listening exercise.   *24 min.*

2   Give participants three minutes each to talk to their partner on a given theme, then three minutes to listen to their partner talking on the same theme. The theme will be one of the six situations listed at the end of the exercise. Begin with the first. When the three minutes are up, ask the partners to swap roles.

3   All those in the inner circle now move round one chair to their right. Tell the group the second situation. Repeat the timed talking and listening process. When both the pair have spoken, the outer circle should move one chair to their right, and greet their new partner.

4   The process continues: after each round the circles take it in turns to move to their right, and the situation changes.

Feedback and discussion   Participants might consider the following questions. How did it feel to be listened to with attention? How often do you give that attention to others? What does power mean to you? What *negative* power have you experienced or exerted? What is *positive* power, and how have you experienced or exerted it?   *6 min.*

Notes   This exercise focuses on the difference between power that is exerted *over* someone (negative power) and power from *within* (positive power), our personal strength which enables us to choose and control the direction of our lives. The exercise could also be used with another set of situations. It is

a structured way of facilitating paired listening work, and avoids the problem of constantly having to find new partners. The structure provides boundaries within which it is safe to talk about difficult subjects. You may want to speed up the exercise, either by cutting the time limit on each exchange or by reducing the number of situations.

Skills   Listening without expressing judgments. Listening with full attention. Verbal expression.

Situations

a   A time when someone had power over you and you felt unable to do anything about it.

b   A time when you had power over someone else and used it badly.

c   A time when you had power and used it well.

d   A time when you felt scared but acted despite your fear.

e   A time when someone had power over you and you stood up to it.

f   A time when you felt helpless, then suddenly knew what to do and did it.

Exercise 7.3 *Time: 25 min.*

STATUES OF POWER

Description A physical exercise, in pairs, using tableaux.

Aims To look at the emotions we associate with power and how they affect us.

Directions

1 Divide the group into pairs. Each pair is going to produce a tableau (frozen image) showing one person in a position of power and the other in a powerless position. Allow them a few minutes to prepare their tableau, then ask them to swap round (so that the powerful figure becomes the powerless and *vice versa*) and prepare a second tableau. *10 min.*

2 When they have prepared both tableaux, give each pair the opportunity to show them to the rest of the group. Ask for quick comments about what people observe. Ask each of the pair in the statue to express what they are feeling in one word (proud, scared, humble, or whatever). *10 min.*

Feedback and discussion Which of the two positions felt more familiar to participants? Can they relate any of the emotions they felt to situations in their lives? What did they feel for the powerless person when they were in the powerful position, and *vice versa*? *5 min.*

Notes This exercise can activate strong associations and emotions quickly, and it is advisable to be conscious of this. Those who have strong emotional reactions might welcome an opportunity to talk about them, in which case it can be a good idea to have feedback in small groups.

Skills Visualisation. Physical expression. Observation.

Exercise 7.4 *Time: 25 min.*

TAKING CONTROL

Description A group exercise looking at ways of using our own power within group and social situations.

Aims To explore ways of taking control or feeling in control. To rehearse these ideas in front of the group. To increase confidence. To find more appropriate ways of presenting oneself.

Directions

1 As a warm-up, ask participants to lie on the ground. Ask them to imagine that they are feeling absolutely useless, with no resources, no confidence, no control. Then, slowly, they rise and start to feel better about themselves. They move up a scale from 1 (feeling absolutely useless, no control) to 10 (confident and totally in control). Everyone walks round the room, slowly changing as they move up their scale. When everyone has reached their 10 you can stop. You could ask a few members to demonstrate their movement from 1 to 5, others from 10 to 5, and a third group from 5 to 10. How often do they feel they do this in everyday life? What do they feel as they move up or down the scale? *10 min.*

2 With everyone in a circle, ask one person at a time to enter the circle and to take control, to feel confident, to have a presence in the group. It is a good idea to create two gaps in the circle, one entry and one exit point. Each individual must decide for themselves what kind of control they want to exercise and how they will establish it. They might, for example:

* Enter the circle quietly, pause, look round the circle, making eye contact with everyone, and depart quietly.
* Rush in and with great excitement tell us what they have seen.
* Come in with confidence, look at one person and request that they move from their chair to an empty chair at the other side of the circle. (The request will be followed if it is issued with the necessary control and authority.)

These are three very different ways of taking control, each of which would suit a different personality, but they are all effective. *10 min.*

Feedback and discussion   What difficulties did participants encounter when attempting to take control? How did they overcome them? What kind of comment or observation from the group would they find useful? Did people get any new ideas from watching the range of approaches? What would members like to practise or improve?   *5 min.*

Notes   Some members might need a lot of challenging and help. A good way is to sit on a chair in the middle of the circle and challenge the member to make you move. Move only when you feel they have achieved the necessary control and authority. Stay seated, giving them tips to improve, until you feel you really would shift!

Skills   Improvisation. Interaction. Exploration. Giving support.

Exercise 7.5   *Time: 40 min.*

POSITIVE AND NEGATIVE THOUGHTS

Description   An advanced communication exercise in groups of six, exploring how our thought patterns can undermine or empower us.

Aims   To explore how our thoughts can influence self-presentation and decision-making. To practise ways of working with both our confident and our doubting sides. To build on work done in Exercise 3.16.

Directions

1   It would be a good idea to have already done Exercise 3.16. Many of the same skills and methods are involved in this exercise.

Groups of six are perfect for this exercise. Do not worry if there are one or two participants left out – it is valuable to have observers who can give feedback. Each group of six divides itself into two groups of three. In one group we have character A, with the two other members representing opposed elements of that character's personality. One plays A's positive and confident thoughts and feelings; the other plays A's negative and doubting thoughts and feelings. The second group divides in a similar way around character B.
5 min.

2   Suggest a situation between characters A and B. (For example, A works for B and is asking for more money). The two teams of three can prepare together. Each draws up a list of the strengths in the arguments of their character, as well as the weak points and the fears of the character.   *10 min.*

3   The procedure is as follows. Character A begins the dialogue, but does not speak until the two assistants have fed them with thoughts (as in Exercise 3.16). Then B can reply, but only when their thoughts have been fed in. The two characters address each other all the time. The assistants are merely voices in their heads. The dialogue stops when A and B think they have come to a dead end, or when they have some resolution.   *15 min.*

Feedback and discussion   How have you coped in situations in which you have felt under internal pressure? Which aspect of your thought processes is dominant? Do these thought

Session 8

processes differ according to situations? How can you take control of these thought processes? When do your thoughts lead you astray? When do your thoughts help you? What patterns can you recognise in your thought processes?

10 min.

Notes The aim of the thoughts is to put pressure on the character. We then need to see how the character deals with these pressures coming from within. The group could work with a far more pressurised situation than the one suggested above. Once members are familiar with the format and techniques, they might, for example, explore a situation in which A is trying to persuade his old friend B to sell some drugs, and B is short of money but has just completed a prison sentence.

When members are comfortable with the exercise, the strict order suggested above could be eased up, with voices intervening at random. The group could also miss out the preparation stages and go straight into the situation. Thus the situation would become totally improvised.

Before the group tackles an A–B dialogue, it is a good idea to do some preparatory work. For example, after the initial preparation described in stage 2 above, the two teams of three could work separately for a while, trying to hold a conversation. The two thoughts would converse only with the character and not between themselves. The character would then reply to them. Group members could choose subjects that they are presently struggling with. Five minutes could be allocated for this.

Skills Teamwork. Judgment. Listening. Concentration. Clarity. Decision-making. Improvisation. Timing.

Introduction Assertiveness – expressing feelings and exploring positive responses; acknowledging and addressing personal and group commitments and needs.   *10 min.*

8.6	ATTACK AND AVOID	*30 min.*
8.7	'I' STATEMENTS	*40 min.*
8.8	MANIPULATIVE TRICKS	*20 min.*
8.9	BILL OF ASSERTIVE RIGHTS	*20 min.*
8.10	NEGOTIATING GROUND RULES	*20 min.*

Reflection   *10 min.*

Notes Exercise 8.6 introduces the theme of assertiveness, exploring the differences between assertive and unassertive behaviour. Exercise 8.7 explores and gives participants an opportunity to develop assertive responses to difficult situations. Exercise 8.8 explores ways of dealing with manipulative behaviour in an assertive way. Exercises 8.9 and 8.10 explore personal and group commitments. They also encourage the group to work out practical guidelines to facilitate group procedure and disputes.

Exercise 8.6   *Time: 30 min.*

ATTACK AND AVOID

Description   A group exercise introducing assertiveness, looking at aggressive and defensive behaviour.

Aims   To gain an understanding of what unassertive behaviour is. To recognise the kinds of behaviour which are familiar to us. To remind ourselves of verbal and body language clues which warn us of an attitude or type of behaviour in others. To notice these signs in ourselves and use them as an opportunity to recognise what kind of response we are likely to use and check that it is appropriate.

Directions

1   Ask participants to fill in Handout 8.6, ATTACKING AND AVOIDING (page 80). How often do they find themselves responding in any of the ways listed on the sheet?   *5 min.*

2   Show where the line is drawn between attacking and avoiding behaviour (between *Revenge* and *Withdrawal*) and ask everyone to note whether their behaviour is more frequently one or the other. Are their ticks concentrated in the upper half (attacking) or the lower half (avoiding)?   *1 min.*

3   Brainstorm the word *attack*, and then the word *avoid*, allowing one minute for each word, with the focus on what they mean for the participants. Use a separate large sheet of paper for each of the two words. Use only half of the sheet at this stage, as you will need space later on.   *2 min.*

4   You have determined what behaviour each word denotes. Ask individual participants to think of one personal reason why they would behave in each of those ways. Under the heading *Why?*, record responses on the appropriate brainstorm sheet. (If you have a large group, you could take a sample.)   *3 min.*

5   Ask individuals to consider how each of these behaviours would be expressed – what they would say, how they would say it, and how they would express it physically. Under the heading *How?*, record the responses.   *3 min.*

6   Ask everyone to think of one word or phrase that they use when either avoiding or attacking, whichever is their most frequent behaviour. They should consider how it is said and the body language which accompanies it. An example of avoiding behaviour could be 'It doesn't matter', said in a way which indicates that it *does* matter, and accompanied by shrugging shoulders and turning away of the head.   *3 min.*

7   Ask somebody to give theirs as a practical example. You might point out how the effect of what they *say* is very largely dependent on what they *do* – their body language. With the 'It doesn't matter' example, you could suggest that they try using the phrase without shrugging their shoulders, and looking straight at the person they are speaking to. This will often have an effect on what they say and the message that is being communicated. In this example, the person may find that when they stop shrugging their shoulders and look straight ahead what they actually want to say is 'It *does* matter'.

In groups of three, get everyone to give their example while the other two in their group offer suggestions about how they might alter their body language to make their response an assertive rather than an attacking or avoiding one.   *7 min.*

Feedback and discussion   What signs can help us to recognise and even predict others' behaviour? What signs can we learn to recognise in ourselves which warn us that we are embarking on an unassertive approach? How can we alter our pattern of reacting and begin to learn a new response? How does it feel to change your body position?   *6 min.*

Notes   Assertiveness has as much to do with body language as with what we say. And what we say is often unconsciously influenced by our own body language. If we adopt defensive physical postures, we are unlikely to speak assertively. On the other hand, if we adopt assertive body language, this can make it easier for us to speak assertively.

An assertive response is a centred response. We are balanced – not leaning forward in an attack mode, not teetering backwards in an avoiding mode. Although most of our confrontations are verbal rather than physical, there are often visual signs, even if they are tiny, of our body going on the attack or the defence. This exercise is a step towards using the signs we get and building up a desired response rather than an immediate reaction.

Skills   Quick thinking. Self-awareness. Investigation.

ATTACKING AND AVOIDING

Behaviour	RARELY	SOMETIMES	FREQUENTLY
NAGGING			
SHOUTING			
INTERRUPTING			
EXPLODING			
WARNING (*IF YOU DON'T DO THIS!*)			
CORRECTING (*LOOK AT THE FACTS!*)			
PERSISTING (*I AM RIGHT!*)			
INSULTING (*YOU'RE PATHETIC!*)			
SARCASM			
REVENGE (*I'LL GET YOU BACK FOR THIS!*)			
WITHDRAWAL			
SULKING IN SILENCE			
TAKING IT OUT ON THE WRONG PERSON			
DECLARING THAT YOU ARE BEING UNFAIRLY TREATED			
TALKING BEHIND SOMEONE'S BACK			
TRYING TO FORGET ABOUT THE PROBLEM			
FEELING ILL			
NOT WANTING TO HURT THE OTHER PERSON			
FEELING LOW AND DEPRESSED			
BEING POLITE BUT FEELING ANGRY			

Exercise 8.7 *Time: 40 min.*

'I' STATEMENTS

Description   An exercise which explains and demonstrates an assertive way of expressing feelings about a problem.

Aims   To show how it is possible to face someone with whom you have a problem without either antagonising them or withdrawing from the problem. To practise making non-judgmental statements, and using a structure which can open rather than close discussion of a difficulty.

Directions

1   Introduce the idea to the group using Handout 8.7 (page 82). This includes examples of clear and clean 'I' statements that have worked.   *15 min.*

2   With the participants in pairs, ask them to prepare one 'I' statement each, relating to a current or recurring difficulty within their work. Partners can help each other to make their statements clear and clean.   *10 min.*

3   Get a few examples from the participants, giving people an opportunity to comment on them and to offer suggestions as to how they might be improved.   *10 min.*

Feedback and discussion   In what ways could the 'I' statement formula be useful to participants? What do they think about it?   *5 min.*

Notes   This is a useful way of separating feelings and facts in order to clarify what a problem really is. The formula may seem stilted and unfamiliar, but with practice it can become an unconscious reaction rather than a laboured response. It is a tough discipline and needs practice.

Groups, as well as individuals, can use the formula to help them make a statement about something they feel strongly about. For example: 'When we can't get up the stairs to the shopping centre we feel angry and frustrated, and we'd like our needs to be taken into consideration when buildings are planned.' It can be a good way for a group to focus their feelings and needs into a coherent statement, for presentation to relevant authorities or audiences.

Skills   Separating feelings from facts. Clarity of expression. Sensitivity. Judgment.

Exercise 8.8 *Time: 20 min.*

MANIPULATIVE TRICKS

Description   An interactive group exercise exploring how to give assertive responses under pressure.

Aims   To practise facing manipulation and finding assertive responses. To apply skills from the previous two exercises.

Directions

1   The MANIPULATION CARDS (see page 83) outline situations in which one person is trying to manipulate another into doing something they don't want to do. Give each participant a card to work with. (You should have copied and cut them in advance.) Allow a short time for participants to decide, individually, what their opening manipulative line will be. If my card says that a parent is trying to persuade their daughter or son to come and visit them, my opening line might be: 'You haven't been to see me for ages. I'm beginning to wonder whether you care about me at all any more.'   *5 min.*

2   Participants return to the circle, and one by one each turns to the person on their left and states very briefly the relationship and the situation on the card – such as 'I am your parent and I want to persuade you to come and visit me.' They then state their opening line and the person on their left makes a response, trying to state their position without rising to the 'bait'. For example, in response to the statement above: 'I have a deadline to meet at work so it's difficult for me to get away at the moment, but let's arrange to spend some time together as soon as it's over.' Give everyone the chance to use their own line and respond to someone else's.   *10 min.*

Feedback and discussion   Which responses are most effective and why? How did people deal with the 'bait' they were offered? How do they usually respond to similar situations? What could they do differently?   *5 min.*

Notes   This exercise draws on work done in Exercises 8.6 and 8.7. The response people are aiming for is one which does not compromise them and which allows them to state their position without resentment or inappropriate anger. They should face the problem, but without attacking or avoiding.

Skills   Improvisation. Imagination. Clear verbal expression.

Information sheet: 'I' statements

An 'I' statement is a way of expressing clearly your point of view about a situation. It includes an expression of how it is affecting you, and how you would like to see it change. The best 'I' statement is free of expectations and blame. It opens up the area for discussion and leaves the next move for the other person.

Aim for your 'I' statement to be *clear* (that is, to the point) and *clean* (that is, free of blame and judgment).

Beware of 'You' statements which place blame on someone else, hold them responsible, demand change from them or hold a threat. For example: 'When you deliberately clump around the house when everyone else is asleep, you are being defiant and disrespectful and you have got to stop doing it before things get really out of hand.'

'I' statement formula

The action A statement of fact. Make it as objective and specific as possible: 'When you run down the stairs with boots on' rather than 'When you're banging around the house'. The objective formulation carries no blame and allows no possibility of denial from the other person.

My response This should be worded in such a way as to acknowledge the subjectivity of your emotions ('I feel angry, hurt, put down, ignored') or the way you want to act ('I feel like giving up').

It should be clear that these feelings carry no blame and impose no expectations on the other person. Say 'I feel hurt' rather than 'I feel that you're being mean'. Add a reason if it helps to clarify the situation for both of you: 'I feel hurt because I enjoy seeing you'.

What I'd like is A statement of a desired change or preferred outcome, but without expectation of change from the other person. It is OK to say what you want, but not to demand it. Say 'What I'd like is to make arrangements that it's possible for us both to keep' rather than 'I'd like you to stop cancelling meetings with me'.

Examples of clean 'I' statements

1 When fed up about others not washing up their coffee cups at the end of each day: 'When I arrive in the morning and see dirty coffee cups on the table I feel frustrated, and what I'd like is to organise a washing-up rota.'

2 When feeling irritable about sharing a double desk with a colleague who isn't tidy: 'When your papers spread over to my side of the desk I feel cramped, and what I'd like is for us to decide where the separating line is so I know how much space I've got.'

3 Youth worker annoyed by club members taking drugs on the premises: 'When you break the rules I feel anxious about the welfare of the club as a whole, and what I'd like is for everyone to share responsibility for keeping the rules.'

4 Youth worker to young people continually interrupting a girls' football session: 'When you walk into the room in the middle of a session I feel disappointed at not being able to finish the work I want to do, and what I'd like is to arrange a time when you could have the room to yourselves.'

5 Youth worker annoyed about colleague arriving late and having to run the club single-handed in the meantime: 'When I'm alone in the club at the start of the evening I feel anxious and uneasy, and what I'd like is not to open the club until there are enough youth workers to cover it.'

Notes

This is a structured format and may seem strange to start with. It takes time to absorb new skills and begin to use them unconsciously. Adapt the language to suit your situation. Use it to extend your understanding of situations you are unhappy about, even if you don't want to say it.

MANIPULATION CARDS

ASKING A FRIEND TO BABYSIT

SMOULDERING
8.8

SUPERVISOR GIVING EXTRA WORK TO WORKER

SMOULDERING
8.8

GETTING SOMEONE TO TAKE OVER YOUR DOOR DUTY IN THE YOUTH CLUB

SMOULDERING
8.8

PARENT PERSUADING DAUGHTER OR SON TO VISIT

SMOULDERING
8.8

GETTING SOMEONE TO GIVE YOU A LIFT HOME

SMOULDERING
8.8

GETTING SOMEONE TO MAKE A TRICKY PHONE CALL FOR YOU

SMOULDERING
8.8

ASKING A FRIEND OR MEMBER OF YOUR FAMILY TO LEND YOU MONEY

SMOULDERING
8.8

BORROWING SOMETHING FROM A FRIEND WHEN THEY DON'T WANT TO LEND IT

SMOULDERING
8.8

GETTING A COLLEAGUE TO MAKE AN UNPLEASANT ANNOUNCEMENT IN THE YOUTH CLUB

SMOULDERING
8.8

PERSUADING A FRIEND TO COME OUT FOR THE EVENING

SMOULDERING
8.8

Exercise 8.9 *Time: 20 min.*

BILL OF ASSERTIVE RIGHTS

Description Small-group work on the rights of the individual, using spoken and written language.

Aims To explore our rights as people. To express what we feel we need. To affirm what we value in ourselves and others. To recognise when we abuse our own rights. To establish a basis for assertiveness. To recognise other people's need to be respected.

Directions

1 Introduce the exercise with examples of assertive rights: for example, the right to be listened to, or the right to my own space.   *2 min.*

2 Tell the group that a bill of assertive rights will be drawn up. Individually each person writes down what they consider their most important right.   *3 min.*

3 Individuals share their suggestions with the whole group. Pin up the rights on which there is agreement. Give an example of how we abuse our own rights: when we assume no-one wants to listen to us and we just keep quiet, we abuse our right to be listened to.   *10 min.*

Feedback and discussion What effect does it have on us when we abuse our own rights or allow others to abuse them? How can we uphold our rights? What effect will this have on others?   *5 min.*

Notes This work is effective when done in conjunction with the work on ground rules in Exercise 8.10, covering the needs and rights of both individuals and groups.

Skills Expressing needs. Acknowledging the needs of others.

Exercise 8.10 *Time: 20 min.*

NEGOTIATING GROUND RULES

Description A group exercise using consensus decision-making to draw up a set of ground rules for the group.

Aims To establish what behaviour is acceptable and unacceptable within the group. To reach consensus about a code of behaviour for the group.

Directions

1 Introduce the exercise: you are all going to work together for a day or weekend, and must establish a set of mutually agreed rules. What kind of behaviour will help things? How do you expect to treat others? How do you expect to be treated by them? What does this entail? Brainstorm suggestions from the group, and record them on a large sheet of paper. Add any of your own that you want to.   *4 min.*

3 Ask everyone to underline any rules they disagree with. They must be prepared to argue the point if they underline anything.   *2 min.*

4 Take a different-coloured pen and circle any rules that have not been underlined. Discuss the least contentious rules first, those underlined only once or twice. Go through all the suggestions, confirming or deleting each rule, by agreement, until you come up with a workable set for the group.   *9 min.*

Feedback and discussion How will the rules be enforced? Should there be penalties for breaking them? How easy or hard will it be to stick to them? How will they benefit you? And others? How will they restrict you? And others?   *5 min.*

Notes Breaking rules is a familiar pattern of behaviour for many young people. Having them participate in making the rules can be a first step in getting them to look at this pattern. Making ground rules is an ongoing process and could become a source of discussion over the day or workshop. The distinction between assertive rights and ground rules can be compared to the distinction between the constitution of a country (the bill of rights) and the laws (ground rules) which are made to uphold it.

Skills Listening. Building on the ideas of others. Being flexible. Finding common ground.

Session 9

Exercise 9.11   *Time: 50 min.*

SITUATIONS ONE TO FIVE

Introduction   Assertiveness in action; locating smouldering situations and working for appropriate responses.   *10 min.*

Notes   Exercise 9.11 gives an opportunity to put assertiveness skills into practice, using situations from participants' lives. Exercises 9.12 and 9.13 explore smouldering situations through the creation of tableaux. Participants will use the information discovered in the exercise to work on strategies for resolution. Exercises 9.14 and 9.15 explore power, status, and ways of transforming our position in any given situation. It is suggested that trainers choose to do *either* 9.12 and 9.13 *or* 9.14 and 9.15, as a set. Each pair runs for 80 minutes.

Description   Interactive group exercise exploring solutions for situations in which individuals find it difficult to be assertive.

Aims   To allow participants to create for themselves a picture of where their difficulties lie, and determine a point at which assertiveness work could effectively begin. To explore what is needed for individuals to be assertive in their situations. To practise assertiveness skills.

Directions

1   Ask participants to divide a blank sheet of paper into five columns marked 1 to 5. Ask them to think of a situation at work where they have found it very difficult to be assertive and cope as they would like to – a situation that they would regard as a really tough problem. It could be either a one-off event or a recurrent difficulty. They mark this down against number 5. Against number 1, ask them to write down something that they feel slightly uncomfortable about dealing with. Against 2, 3 and 4 they should write down other problematic situations, grading them from the minor difficulty of number 1 to the major dilemma of number 5.

5 min.

2   In groups of three, each person shares one of their problems from lists 1 to 5. Encourage them to choose something nearer 1 than 5. To take on the hardest problem at this stage is not a good way to build up confidence and self-esteem.   *5 min.*

3   Each group enacts each of the three situations as they happened or might happen. Everyone should be given the opportunity to work on their own situation.   *15 min.*

4   The enacted scenes are shared with the whole group (or, if the whole group is large, with another group of three). Watch the first scene, then find out the *priority* and the *desired outcome* for the person involved (see the notes). Ask for suggestions from the observers as to how they could achieve the latter without abandoning the former. It is important that these suggestions are framed in a supportive way and are not judgmental or critical. Remind people to watch out for body language and other encoded messages, verbal as well as non-verbal. Once suggestions have been made, the scenes can be replayed all the way through with the altered, and hopefully more assertive, behaviour.   *20 min.*

Feedback and discussion Participants might consider the following questions. What is your priority in each situation? What is your desired outcome? Can you achieve your desired outcome without compromising your priority? What will people take away with them from this exercise? What was useful to them? What advice or suggestions were helpful and why? What made it difficult and why?   *5 min.*

Notes An example might help to clarify the distinction between *priority* and *desired outcome*. A friend has given Sarah a birthday present she doesn't like. Her priority is not to hurt her friend's feelings. Her desired outcome is to take the present back and change it. If she feels she will hurt her friend's feelings in the process, she does not want to take the present back. Assertiveness in this instance does not mean taking the present back regardless. She must acknowledge her priorities and work with them, not against them. Is there any way in which she can achieve the desired outcome without sacrificing her priorities, and without dishonesty?

Use the exercise to build confidence, and practise using earlier voice or body language exploration to find an assertive response.

Skills Clarity. Self-awareness and awareness of others. Improvisation. Assertiveness.

SMOULDERING IN THE FAMILY

Description Interactive physical exercise in small groups, examining points of friction and tension in the family.

Aims To draw a picture of tensions and potential difficulties in family life. To look at how we can recognise smouldering in our own lives.

Directions

1 Divide into small groups. Involving the other members of their group, each participant in turn creates a tableau of what family life means to them. They should use words only to explain how they want the others to position themselves. If a participant can relate to someone else's picture and it needs only a slight alteration to make it represent their own experience, they should ask them to make the alteration rather than creating a whole new picture.   *10 min.*

2 Each group should produce one final tableau which contains elements that everyone can relate to. If there are opposing interpretations of family life which cannot be contained in one picture, then they should produce one picture for each viewpoint. Ask each figure what they are feeling. Their answer should be given in one word – angry, sad, happy, or whatever.   *15 min.*

3 As a whole group, look at the final tableaux. What tensions or difficulties do you observe? Where are the potential points of conflict? What, if anything, is smouldering in each picture?   *10 min.*

Feedback and discussion What kinds of action could be taken to move difficult and tense situations forward to possible solutions?   *5 min.*

Notes Using tableaux or 'still pictures' allows for two types of interpretation. Participants can produce either a 'photograph' (a realistic image, a 'scene' from family life) or an abstract representation of their feelings and understanding. (An abstract representation of family harmony, for instance, might involve the participants standing in a circle with their hands joined.) Both styles are welcome in this exercise, but it is helpful if you as facilitator can make this distinction both in introducing the work and in interpreting it.

Looking at what family means to us is a powerful way of exploring some of our fundamental differences and similarities. This work can be used with culturally mixed groups as a way of sharing the different perceptions and expectations we have grown up with, and how that affects our understanding and experience of conflict. The next exercise looks at community in the same way.

Skills   Physical expression. Co-operation. Creative building on ideas. Observation.

SMOULDERING IN THE COMMUNITY

Description   Interactive physical exercise in small groups, examining points of friction and tension in the community.

Aims   To create a tableau which represents our view of our communities. To look for tension and potential conflict in the tableau. To experience and use visual communication.

Directions

1   Divide into three groups. Each group takes one of the following areas: in the workplace; at leisure; on the streets. Each group produces one tableau on their subject. It can be set in one place, such as an office or factory, or it can be a montage of individual tableaux – for example, one person in a shop, one as a nurse, one as a gardener, etc. Groups decide for themselves what is appropriate.   *20 min.*

2   The whole group looks at each of the community tableaux. Ask each person who they are, how they are feeling, what they are doing. What frictions or tensions does the group observe? What are the areas of potential conflict?   *15 min.*

Feedback and discussion   How can you anticipate difficulties within your community and what can you do about them? What kind of intervention is possible or desirable?   *5 mins.*

Notes   Ask questions which will reveal more about what goes on behind the immediate picture. A tableau of leisure activity in the community, for example, can reveal a surprising variety of information: a tableau of a dry ski-slope in use might raise questions about who uses it, and reveal that it is used wholly by people from outside the community; or a tableau of a woman drinking in a pub might raise questions about provision of public transport and the dangers of the streets after dark.

Skills   Physical expression. Co-operation. Observation. Creative building on ideas.

Exercise 9.14 *Time: 30 min.*

POSITIONAL VERSUS PERSONAL POWER

Description   Structured role-play exercise exploring the difference between power and status.

Aims   To explore the differences and similarities between positional and personal power, and between confidence and assertiveness.

Directions

1   Divide participants into groups of three. Ask each group to think of a clear line of positional power between three people – for example, from the president to the secretary to the cleaner. On a scale of 1 to 10, the person at the top of the power structure is a 10, the person at the bottom a 1, and the third person somewhere in between.

Agree a message to be passed from the top to the bottom, and a response to be passed from the bottom to the top. For example, the president tells the secretary to make sure the office is cleaned by the time work begins each day, and the secretary therefore tells the cleaner to get to work earlier; the cleaner makes a response to the secretary, who passes this on to the president.

Each group practises the passing of the downward and upward messages. When everyone is clear about their positional power, the second stage of the role-play can be introduced.   *10 min.*

2   The line of positional power and the substance of the messages remain the same, but the characters' personal power, or assertiveness, is inversely proportionate to their positional power. The president retains a positional power of 10, but assumes a personal power of 1 or 2; the cleaner still has a low positional power, but takes on a personal power of 9 or 10. You can either give each group the numbers for their characters' personal power, or they can choose for themselves how they would like to alter it.

The scenes can now be played again, with the same characters and the same messages but with the new hierarchy of personal power. If you are working with a group which enjoys drama, you might invite everyone to watch each group play the two versions of their scene. There can be great comedy in the contrast.   *10 min.*

Feedback and discussion   What is the difference between positional and personal power? What characterises each? What differences do participants perceive when they are on the receiving end of each of these kinds of power? Can they identify aspects of both positional and personal power in the people they work with? How are they used?   *10 min.*

Notes   This exercise allows participants to try out different levels of personal power and to discover the effect that it can have on the course of events. It is encouraging to witness the fact that someone in a low position can assert themselves and thereby exercise a certain power of their own.

Skills   Role-play. Improvisation. Co-operation.

Exercise 9.15   *Time: 50 min.*

CHANGING THE OUTCOME

Description   Tableau work in small groups focusing on changing the position of the powerless in a given situation.

Aims   To explore the experience of feeling powerless. To express it visually. To try out alternatives and see their effect.

Directions

1   Ask participants to think individually of one incident in which they felt powerless and unable to do anything about it. It could be a situation that they tried but failed to change, or one in which they would have liked to achieve a different outcome.   *5 min.*

2   In groups of three, each person in turn silently sculpts the rest of their group into three tableaux that depict the beginning, the middle and the end of the situation. (For *sculpting*, see page 16.) It is necessary to tell people who they are only if they are confused about what they are representing in the tableau.   *10 min.*

3   When all the groups have produced the set of tableaux for each of their members, they choose one of the stories to work on. Run the sequence of tableaux again for the chosen story, this time incorporating one spoken thought for each of the characters – that is, one thought in each tableau. The thoughts should be spoken in a predetermined order.   *10 min.*

4   Working on the same story, extend the tableaux and thoughts into three short scenes – no more than a minute for each one. Each person turns their thought into a sentence, combining it with some appropriate physical action.   *5 min.*

5   Come back to the whole group and see the work from each subgroup. Choose one of the subgroups to use in a demonstration. Take a tableau which has an easily identifiable oppressor, and an oppressed person with whom we can feel sympathy. Ask the rest of the participants to suggest how the powerless person might act to alter the situation. Try out these suggestions, with the participant who has the new idea going into the piece and playing the person whose actions they want to change. Continue this process with each of the stories, either as one group or with two of the groups joining together and serving as an audience for each other.   *15 min.*

Feedback and discussion   *What is the effect of different actions on the outcome? How does the exercise relate to the lives of participants? What can they take away with them from this work?*   *5 min.*

Notes   This exercise links with earlier work on assertiveness in Exercises 4.3 and 9.11. It is important that the group works on creative alternatives to the powerless response, rather than merely criticising it. A group will often be able to see solutions that the individual does not see.

Skills   Visualising. Creative thinking. Expression.

FANNING THE FLAMES

Anger, enemies and awareness

FANNING THE FLAMES

Anger, enemies and awareness

The smouldering coals lie still, ready either to ignite or to die down. Bellows blow, and the still coals flicker with life. The wind blows relentlessly, giving life to the fire. The flames lick, leap and grow. The fire has taken hold. There is no longer a possibility that it will fade.

THE potential for conflict is about to be realised. There are provokers who will not let go, who will not let things lie. They push on, persist, irritate and inflame: they take the bellows and blow. Urging the fire to take on is important for provokers. There are needs and hurts that will not die down or fade away. There is too much anger and hurt for some involved in the conflict to let go. They feel a need to maintain distrust, and to nurture feelings of prejudice or hate. At this stage a mediator could intervene and offer a forum for the expression of these difficult emotions. A conflagration can still be averted, but it is becoming increasingly difficult.

Focus   Expressing, receiving, and containing anger. Prejudice, projection and enmity.

Aims   To develop skills for getting to the root of anger, both our own and others'. To explore the idea that we create enemies and opposition by projecting the unacceptable aspects of ourselves onto others. To explore the emotions and needs that we repress and project onto others. To develop skills for meeting these things in others.

Key concepts   Anger – hurt, needs and fears; enemies and projection; prejudice and fear; bitterness and resentment.

Key questions   What lies at the root of our own anger? What lies at the root of the anger we receive from others? What lies at the root of our hate and prejudice? What do our 'enemies' and our scapegoats represent?

This section contains three two-and-a-half-hour sessions. Session 10 deals with personal anger – facing it in ourselves and others. Session 11 looks at facing the anger of others, expressing strong feelings in a group context and working towards an agreeable resolution. Session 12 focuses on enemies – who they are, why we create them – and projection, of ourselves onto others and *vice versa*. It also deals with prejudice, and how to face it.

All training techniques (such as brainstorm, role-play and tableau work) are explained in TRAINING FOR TRAINERS.

Session 10

Introduction Personal anger, facing your own anger, facing the anger of others.   *10 min.*

10.1	STATEMENTS ON ANGER	*25 min.*
10.2	EMOTION PICTURES	*15 min.*
10.3	STATUES OF ANGER	*20 min.*
10.4	UNDERLYING ANGER	*20 min.*
10.5	YES/NO	*10 min.*
10.6	DOUBLE ANGER	*40 min.*

Reflection   *10 min.*

Notes Exercise 10.1 is an introductory exercise on anger. Exercise 10.2 explores physical representations of anger and other emotions. Exercise 10.3 continues the work of the second, this time concentrating on the concepts of anger and hate, hurt and bitterness. Exercise 10.4 uses a scheme to help us get beneath anger and begin to address its causes. Exercise 10.5 is a short physical warm-up for the following exercise. Exercise 10.6 is a practical exercise in which participants apply the skills learnt in Exercise 10.4.

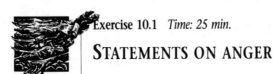

Exercise 10.1   *Time: 25 min.*

STATEMENTS ON ANGER

Description An individual writing exercise looking at different ways of expressing anger and attitudes towards it.

Aims To provoke thoughts about learned personal attitudes to anger. To recognise the messages about anger that we grew up with, and to look at how they influence us.

Directions

1 Ask participants to think about their parents' attitude towards anger. (For 'parents', take the two most influential adults in their lives when they were growing up – for example, mother, father, guardian, grandparents, teachers.) What did they hear them say about anger? How did their parents express their anger? What sums up their attitude? Get each participant to write a brief description (one or two sentences) of the point of view of one of their parents. For example: 'My mother didn't like anger. She thought it was an unnecessary display of emotion, and would rather not see it expressed.' If they can think of something actually said to them by that parent, they should write that down too. For example: 'My mother often said "I'm not angry. I want everyone to be happy. No-one need be angry."'   *8 min.*

2 They now follow the same idea, but do it for themselves. What do you think about anger? What kinds of things do you say to people when you're angry?   *4 min.*

3 Ask participants to join up with a partner and share as much of their statements as they want to.   *8 min.*

Feedback and discussion Can participants see either of their parents reflected in the way that they themselves express or repress anger? What do they value about what they were taught? Would they like to experience and express their own anger differently? In what way?   *5 min.*

Notes Anger can be experienced and expressed in many different ways. What we see and hear at home has an enormous effect in shaping our understanding of it, and how we feel able to express it. If time is short, stage 2 of the exercise can be omitted.

Skills Reflection. Expression. Self-awareness.

Exercise 10.2   *Time: 15 min.*

EMOTION PICTURES

Description   An exercise using individual tableaux (or 'statues') to brainstorm feelings and reactions to emotions.

Aims   To gain an overall picture of what particular words mean to the group. For participants to express their immediate point of view without words.

Directions

Tell the group that you want to know what particular words mean to them. Emphasise that there is no right or wrong answer – it is the personal understanding of the word that you are after. Ask the group to stand up. Ask them to give their immediate reactions, not their considered responses, to each word you give them. On hearing the word, each person should make an immediate physical picture, using face and body, showing what the word means to them. Use these words: anger, hate, frustration, love, anxiety. With each word, have participants hold the picture, and look around the room to find families of tableaux. For example, 'love' might produce some adoring pictures, some smothering, some sexual, etc. Participants can group themselves together with those who they feel have similar interpretations to their own. You will quickly have a visual impression of what the group feels about the subject.   *10 min.*

Feedback and discussion   Participants might consider the following questions. In what way does your experience of anger affect what the word means to you? What surprised you about what you learned of the reactions of the others? Were you surprised by your own reactions?   *5 min.*

Notes   Although we may speak the same language, our different experiences mean that we have different understandings of the same word. Using statues is an effective way of getting quickly to what a group thinks and feels about key words. For some it is easier to react physically to a word than to respond verbally. Use the feedback time to encourage the group to give their verbal reactions to the words, and explore their differences and similarities.

Skills   Instant reactions. Physical expression. Self-awareness.

Exercise 10.3   *Time: 20 min.*

STATUES OF ANGER

Description   Paired tableau work on aspects of anger.

Aims   To make links between anger and hate, hurt and bitterness. To turn an understanding of an emotion into a visual expression. To raise ideas about both the creative and the destructive power of anger.

Directions

1   Prepare a set of index cards. On half of them write 'anger' on one side, 'hate' and 'aggression' on the other side. On the remaining cards write 'hurt' on one side, 'bitterness' and 'resentment' on the other. Divide the group into pairs. Each pair is given one card, so that half of the group will be working on anger and the other half on hurt. In each pair one person (A) moulds their partner (B) into a statue which expresses the key word.   *5 min.*

2   B moulds A into a statue which expresses the words on the other side of the same card. (If B has been sculpted into an expression of hurt, their task will be to mould A into an expression of resentment or bitterness.)   *5 min.*

3   Pick a few of the pairs of statues to comment on. Look at them as pairs, and encourage observation from the rest of the group. Which statue is expressing which emotion? Ask each statue how they are feeling in their chosen position.   *5 min.*

Feedback and discussion   What connections do you make between hurt and bitterness? What connections do you make between anger and hate? In what ways do you see anger as a destructive emotion? In what ways might it be used positively?   *5 min.*

Notes   Often when we are hurt we push away the pain in the hope that it will disappear. We may believe that it has gone, but it sometimes remains in the shape of bitterness or resentment. When anger is unacknowledged and has no outlet, it can turn into aggression or hate. Accumulated anger and hurt, when they finally break out, can be very destructive. But anger itself need not be destructive. You can use this exercise to open up the discussion on anger as a positive force.

Skills   Visualisation. Interpretation. Observation.

Exercise 10.4   *Time: 20 min.*

UNDERLYING ANGER

Description   A written exercise about what underlies anger.

Aims   To encourage participants to consider and express what lay beneath an instance of personal anger.

Directions

1   Ask everyone to write down (in one sentence) a situation at work where they felt really angry. For example: 'I felt angry when my contribution in a meeting was ignored.'   *2 min.*

2   Explain that a layer of hurt very often underlies anger. Ask everyone to write a sentence about the hurt behind their anger in the instance they have thought of. For example: 'I felt hurt because it seemed that nobody valued my opinion.'   *2 min.*

3   The reason for the hurt is often an unmet need. Ask everyone to write a sentence covering their needs in the same instance. For example: 'I need to be accepted and valued by my colleagues.'   *2 min.*

4   Alongside the need are often fears. Ask participants to think about what fears might have lay behind their anger and write a sentence about them. For example: 'I have a fear that I won't be able to win my colleagues' respect.'   *2 min.*

5   Participants turn to a partner and share their sentences with them. If anyone has had difficulty with the exercise, their partner can help them unravel their feelings.   *6 min.*

Feedback and discussion   What is the value of understanding the substructure of anger? In what ways could it help you in your work?   *6 min.*

Notes   Anger and hurt are often two sides of the same coin. It is an important step in facing the anger of others to know what lies beneath our own anger. This exercise is a way of discovering some of the hurt, needs and fears underlying a personal experience of extreme anger. If we can identify the fears that lie at the roots of anger (either our own or others'), we can begin addressing those fears rather than remaining caught up in the outward emotion. This exercise is developed further in Exercises 10.6 and 11.7.

Skills   Uncovering, clarifying and expressing feelings.

Exercise 10.5   *Time: 10 min.*

YES/NO

Description   A physical warm-up exercise exploring experiences of resisting and insisting.

Aims   To remind ourselves of our experiences of resisting and insisting. To prepare for the next exercise.

Directions

1   Form two lines of people down the middle of the room. Everyone sits on the floor with their back to their partner and links arms with them. One of the lines is the YES side, the other the NO side. Each person on the YES side is trying to gain ground; each person on the NO side is trying to maintain their ground and resist the encroachment. Participants remain sitting back-to-back on the floor whilst pushing against each other. The only words they can use are yes and no, according to which side they are on. The two sides should have equal time being YES and being NO.   *3 min.*

2   In the same pairs, standing up and facing each other, participants argue, using only the words yes and no. Again each person should try both sides.   *4 min.*

Feedback and discussion   Ask the following questions. What did it feel like when you were winning or losing? What was your most effective strategy – shouting, speaking firmly, withdrawing? Think about the strategies you use in your life when you are up against what seems to be a hopeless situation. Do they get you the results you want?   *3 min.*

Notes   In the course of this exercise, participants might find themselves recalling (and perhaps drawing inspiration from) specific incidents in which they have played either the YES or the NO part. They should hold on to those memories as reminders of where they need to work on their assertiveness. The exercise can reveal patterns in participants' ability to say yes or no. The work could be developed to explore situations in which participants have particular difficulty, and to help them rehearse ways of saying what they want to say.

Skills   Focus. Quick responses. Imagination. Concentration.

Exercise 10.6 *Time: 40 min.*

DOUBLE ANGER

Description A small-group exercise in which participants apply what was learned in Exercise 10.4, UNDERLYING ANGER.

Aims To practise using the steps in UNDERLYING ANGER in a simulated situation under pressure of time. To see how the knowledge of what we are feeling, and why we are feeling it, affects the way in which we continue a confrontation or argument. To practise careful listening, quick assessment of a given situation, and clear and coherent communication.

Directions

1 You will need to prepare pairs of dispute cards in advance. Groups of five are ideal for this exercise. Two members of each group will become disputants. They will each receive a card, on which is written a brief scenario for the argument about to be improvised. The cards should be conceived as compatible pairs. For example: (1) Your colleague has not consulted you about an important decision and you are furious. (2) Your colleague is always interfering with your work and responsibilities, and this makes you very angry.

Two other members of the group are each attached to one of the disputants as an outside 'adviser'. The fifth member of the group observes the argument and is the caller. *10 min.*

2 The two protagonists now start an argument, using the scenarios on their respective cards. When the caller feels that the dispute has warmed up, they shout 'freeze'. The two advisers now intervene, one at a time, and tell their disputant what they feel to be the *hurt* that is involved. The caller shouts 'action' and the disputants launch into another round of argument. When the caller feels that the dispute has progressed they again shout 'freeze', and this time the advisers tell each of the disputants what they see as the *needs* underpinning the dispute. The caller shouts 'action' again. The protagonists continue with their argument. The caller shouts 'freeze' when appropriate, and again the advisers come in. This time they focus on the *fears* of their respective disputants. The exercise can now be completed, with the option of a final round of argument to see if the advisers' last intervention will influence the disputants in any way. You might have time to swap roles and repeat the exercise. *20 min.*

Feedback and discussion In what way did the information shared between the advisers and disputants actually influence the proceedings? How difficult is it in the 'heat of battle' to make quick and accurate assessments of situations? Did the advisers locate the key underlying elements – the hurt, needs and fears? Did the advisers' comments make sense to the protagonists? Did the caller keep good order and control, and were they sensitive to the needs of the participants and the dynamics of the exercise? *10 min.*

Notes If there is not a fifth member to act as caller, whenever one of the advisers feels they are ready for comment they call 'freeze'. The second adviser has to comment at the same time and they call 'action' when ready. It is more difficult to do the exercise with the advisers as callers, especially if it is the first time the group are attempting it.

The exercise can develop in two different ways. The disputants can choose to ignore the advisers' comments, or even take them as cues for further anger. On the other hand, the advisers' comments can help to inform the combatants, encouraging them to communicate more clearly what is really happening for them rather than concealing their deepest feelings behind the anger.

Skills Listening. Observation. Clarity. Brevity. Acting and thinking under pressure. Role-play and improvisation. Giving appropriate information. Timing. Giving clear instructions.

Session 11

FACING ANGER

Introduction   Facing the anger of others; expressing strong feelings in a group context and working towards an agreeable resolution.   *10 min.*

11.7	FACING ANGER	*55 min.*
11.8	WORDS UNHEARD	*15 min.*
11.9	MIRROR REFLECTION	*20 min.*
11.10	CIRCLE PROBLEM SOLVE	*40 min.*

Reflection   *10 min.*

Notes   Exercise 11.7 is another exercise giving participants experience in facing anger from some other party. Exercise 11.8 is a warm-up for exercise 11.9, which promotes active listening in group discussion and helps to facilitate group communication. Exercise 11.10 is a difficult group problem-solving exercise.

Description   A small-group exercise putting into further practice the ideas and techniques explored in Exercises 10.4 and 10.6.

Aims   To practise receiving someone's anger and helping them transform it into constructive action. To practise planning a strategy before taking action. To practise observation of a partner's performance and the giving of constructive feedback. To practise receiving constructive feedback.

Directions

1   This first stage is to prepare the ground for the rest of the exercise. Ask participants to think of a time when someone unleashed their anger on them. What was said? How were they approached? How did they respond? What do they think their hurt, needs and fears were?   *10 min.*

2   Ask participants to share this remembered situation with a partner. They will then assume the role of the person who unleashed their anger on them. The partner will attempt to locate this character's hurts, needs and fears. Then they swap over and repeat. They should compare notes at the end and see if their thoughts about the hurts, needs and fears of the angry character were alike.   *10 min.*

3   Divide participants into groups of four, each comprising two teams. In the first team we have Anger and an adviser; in the second team we have Receiver and an adviser. Both teams are given a card with a dispute written on it. (The two cards should be the same.) An example could be: *You always thought that you received the same pay as other colleagues. You have recently discovered that this is not so. It has made you very angry.* The angry team decides the identity of the individual that they will approach in order to focus their anger.

The teams now prepare separately. The angry team prepares its opening line while the receiving team, anticipating some of the feelings that might emerge, prepares some possible opening responses.   *10 min.*

4   Anger and Receiver now begin the role-play. Anger starts. Receiver attempts all the time to get behind the anger and to influence the discussion constructively. The two advisers observe closely and monitor how their partners are doing. (Everyone could now swap roles and play the situation again, but extra time might need to be allocated for this.)   *10 min.*

5   In pairs, the participants look at all the techniques and responses that emerged from the role-play. When the pairs have finished, the four can share their comments and observations.   *5 min.*

Feedback and discussion   How did participants feel about their in-role performances? What did they learn by participating and observing? How did the feedback from the observers help the participants to understand what had occurred? Were the teams well prepared, and how much did they have to deviate from their original planning?   *10 min.*

Notes   You could explore the nature of observation. What were the advisers looking for, and why? It is useful to get them to articulate their approach, and see in what way it could be improved. This exercise could also be used for the · development of self-criticism, in pairs or individually.

Skills   Role-play and improvisation. Listening and observation. Clear feedback. Responding under pressure.

Exercise 11.8   *Time: 15 min.*

WORDS UNHEARD

Description   A paired listening exercise introducing the concept of mirror reflection.

Aims   To practise a way of checking that we are listening to, and properly hearing, what another person says.

Directions

1   Divide into pairs. Decide who is A and who is B. The subject in the first round is *What I did yesterday evening*. A and B have two minutes to tell each other what they did. They both speak at the same time, and both concentrate only on the telling. They are not interested in each other's story; they just want to get their own across.   *3 min.*

2   Again give each person two minutes to tell their partner something interesting they did, either yesterday evening or last week. Again the two partners speak simultaneously, but this time they are also trying to listen to each other's story. Allow one minute for quick feedback between partners before moving on to the next stage.   *4 min.*

3   Partner A makes a statement which reflects their personal convictions. For example: 'I think that the devastation of the rainforests is the most important social issue at the moment, and everyone should put their campaigning energies into stopping it.' B sums up what A has said, and continues the discussion with a new statement. Even if they personally agree with it, B's statement should contradict A's. This is a role-play exercise and it works better when there are opposing views. When B has made the replying statement, A sums up what B has just said and makes a reply. The discussion continues in this way, with every statement being summed up before the next point is made.   *4 min.*

Feedback and discussion   Put the following questions to participants. What was familiar to you in the first stages? Are you often listened to without good attention? Do you often listen in that way? What was it like trying to speak and listen at the same time? What did your partner do that made it easier or more difficult to hear what they said? What effect did it have on you when you heard your viewpoint reflected back?   *4 min.*

Exercise 11.8 *Continued*

Notes This exercise is a lead-up to the next one, on active listening. It is very hard to really hear what someone is saying when you are convinced that you disagree, but the practice of it is a valuable discipline. If the group have coped well with this exercise, they will move on to the group version of it without too much resistance. It is advisable to do this exercise first, as moving straight into group discussion with this method is tough and may be rejected.

Skills Verbal articulacy. Doing two things at once. Active and concentrated listening.

Exercise 11.9 *Time: 20 min.*

MIRROR REFLECTION

Description Group discussion exercise involving active listening and reporting back.

Aims To practise active-listening skills in a group. To gain practice in using what is a useful tool for facilitating group discussions.

Directions

Start with everyone seated in a circle. Introduce the exercise as a group discussion which will involve active listening. The subject of the discussion could either be an issue about which people will have many different opinions, or a difficulty of group dynamics which is specific to this group of people. There is one rule which must be stuck to: before anyone makes their own point, they must sum up what the previous speaker has said.

If the previous speaker does not feel that they have been properly heard, the person reporting back must listen and sum up again. Only when the feedback is accepted may they go on to make their own point. In this way every contribution is heard to the satisfaction of the speaker. *15 min.*

Feedback and discussion What did participants learn about their listening habits? How easy did people find it to actually hear what was being said? *5 min.*

Notes It is hard to listen well to someone else's point of view when you are involved in a dispute with them. This exercise demands disciplined listening from everyone involved. It involves a style of listening and feeding back which may well be unfamiliar to the group. Participants will need practice before they will readily be able to use the technique to resolve difficulties in the group. When they do use it, the group may find that mirror reflection not only affirms the value of individuals but quickly reduces misunderstanding.

Skills Active listening – that is, listening and assimilating without judging. Summarising. Feeding back. Clarity.

Exercise 11.10   *Time: 40 min.*

CIRCLE PROBLEM SOLVE

Description   A group problem-solving exercise involving close co-operation and imagination.

Aims   To work creatively towards the resolution of a problem that has been identified. To involve all members of the group in this process. To facilitate the process by applying a disciplined and structured method.

Directions

1   One member of the group is invited to pose a problem to the rest of the group. For example: 'I know we've agreed that the van is a smoke-free zone, but I find it impossible to go the whole journey without a cigarette. I have to be able to smoke.' The group then comes to an agreement that they will co-operatively resolve this problem. (The notion behind the exercise is that the group has a collective interest in the well-being of each of its members. If one member of the group has a problem, and shares it with the others, it therefore becomes a problem for the whole group.)

2   The person to the left of the first speaker has the task of checking the details and clarifying what has been said. This would be done in the second person: 'Mary, you said ... ' The first speaker then confirms that their problem has been accurately heard.

3   The person to the left of the second speaker now opens out the problem to the group, again repeating what the first member said but this time starting with the words: 'A member of the group feels ... ' In this way the original problem is depersonalised and becomes a problem for the whole group to tackle.

4   A fourth group member (the person to the left of the third speaker) now defines the task: 'We need to create a situation in which smokers can have a cigarette when travelling, while at the same time keeping the van a smoke-free zone as has already been agreed.' This speaker then seeks confirmation from the whole group that they agree to the task as proposed. (The speaker who has the responsibility of defining the task should try to suggest an approach which takes into account all sides in the dispute. This is more likely to get the immediate

agreement of the whole group. If agreement is not reached, however, the group might try resolving the issue by using discussion structures covered in *TRAINING FOR TRAINERS*. See pages 25–26.)

5   A fifth group member now makes the first suggestion as to how the problem might be addressed. (It should be a suggestion, not a prescription.)

6   Now proceed round the circle with everyone contributing. The idea is that each contribution should build on what has previously been said, gradually moving the problem towards a solution. This might take more than one complete round of the circle. If someone wants to change the direction in which the solution is developing, they must first reflect back what has already been said, then give their reason for disagreeing, and then make their own new suggestion. In this way, no individual can hijack the decision-making process. The following speaker can choose whether to return to the original group proposals or follow the new suggestion. If a new proposal is adopted and leads to a solution, it is important to get affirmation from the whole group. Some members may not have participated fully in the resolution, and may still wish to pursue an earlier proposal. In this case the present solution should be put on hold while the group explores the earlier proposal, with all agreeing that the focus will be only on the one suggestion.   *30 min.*

Feedback and discussion   What difficulties did the group encounter? What do we need to make the exercise successful? What does the exercise demand from the group?   *10 min.*

Notes   If you do not want it to be possible for one group member to change the course of the exercise, even with the suggested safeguards, you can establish a simple rule that participants can only build on what they have received. This way you will at least have a solution at the end of the round. It might not be one that the whole group supports, which is a drawback, but you can subsequently explore other suggestions using the same model. This structure is less flexible but less complicated, and could be used until the group are sufficiently acquainted with the exercise. Group members may find it useful to have their specific task written on a card in front of them, particularly the first five people in the circle.

This exercise will not work without generosity and close and careful co-operation from all group members. It is difficult to use in a hostile environment. But when a group can solve its problems or difficulties in this way, it feels strong, positive and cohesive. Once the group becomes used to this disciplined structure, the approach becomes automatic and relaxed. The group support, co-operation, attention and focus which the exercise demands are all aspects of the dynamics of a group which is functioning well. The exercise highlights what it takes to work as a group.

Skills Active listening and concentration. Clarity of expression. Active decision-making. Group support and co-operation.

Session 12

Introduction Enemies: who they are and why we create them. Projection: your own and from others. Prejudice. Facing prejudice.   *10 min.*

12.11	ENEMY THINKING	*10 min.*
12.12	MY ENEMY	*30 min.*
12.13	PERSONAL PROJECTION	*20 min.*
12.14	OUTSIDERS	*10 min.*
12.15	FACING PROJECTION FROM OTHERS	*60 min.*

Reflection   *10 min.*

Notes Exercise 12.11 is an introductory brainstorming exercise to find out what 'enemy' means to us. Exercises 12.12 and 12.13 explore personal projection. Exercise 12.14 is a short warm-up for Exercise 12.15, which is an active exercise giving participants a chance to explore and respond to prejudice expressed by another.

Exercise 12.11   *Time: 10 min.*

ENEMY THINKING

Description   A brainstorm to gather ideas and perceptions of what 'enemy' means to the group.

Aims   To gather information about the range of opinions and perceptions within the group without discussion or argument. To establish a starting point for work on enemies and 'enemy thinking'.

Directions

Brainstorm the word 'enemy'. Ask the group what it means to them. What were they taught to think an enemy is? Who were they taught to see as the enemy? What feelings do they associate with the word? What fears do they associate with it? Introduce the idea of 'enemy thinking': for example, 'The enemy are wrong', 'We're better than them', 'They want to hurt us', etc. How do participants think about their enemies? How do we *make* enemies?   *5 min.*

Feedback and discussion   What does 'enemy thinking' and having enemies do to us as a society and individually? What are the similarities and differences in our understandings of what 'enemy' means to us? What do our enemies have in common?   *5 min.*

Notes   This is a brief idea-gathering exercise to encourage participants to see the scope of the work you will be doing on enemies. It is primarily a stimulation exercise to raise questions, and not to answer any. Encourage participants to use one-word and short-phrase contributions to the brainstorm, so that they do not get bogged down trying to explain and justify what they are saying.

Skills   Quick thinking. Free association. Group acceptance of ideas.

Exercise 12.12   *Time: 30 min.*

MY ENEMY

Description   A paired tableau exercise exploring the concept of 'enemy'.

Aims   To examine our enemies. To find links between our enemies and us. To explore threats represented to each by the other.

Directions

1   Ask all participants to write down three things that they hate or fear about their enemy. They should try to think of someone or a group of people they really dislike, either for themselves or for what they represent. If they find it impossible to think in those terms, they can use as an enemy someone or a group of people they were taught to hate or fear as a child.   *5 min.*

2   Put participants into pairs. One partner starts by shaping or sculpting the other into a statue of their enemy. For example, A sculpts B into a statue of a large man in an arrogant pose, smoking a cigar. (For *sculpting*, see page 16.)   *5 min.*

3   B now responds by shaping A into a statue which represents how the statue B might see A. For example, B (as a large man with a cigar) might sculpt A into an ungrateful woman who doesn't know when she's got a good deal. Ask A and B how they feel as a large man with a cigar and an ungrateful woman. What do they gain from this part of the exercise?   *5 min.*

4   Examine a selection of the statues within the group, as pairs. Each completed picture shows us A and B as enemies. We see what they think of each other. Ask each of them, in character, to complete the sentence 'You are my enemy because ... '   *5 min.*

5   Everyone watching looks for common characteristics in the two sculpted characters. What is at the root of their hatred? What threatens them? What do they fear in one another? (For example: A is threatened by B's positional power, and fears his lack of respect; B is threatened by A's personal power, and fears what she represents.)   *5 min.*

6   If you want to change round and give the Bs a chance to sculpt A into their enemy, extra time might be needed.

Feedback and discussion   What do we and our enemies have in common? What fears do we share? What threats do we represent to each other?   *5 min.*

Notes   Carl Jung, an influential psychologist, suggested that we project what we dislike or fear about ourselves onto others and dissociate ourselves from it, thereby creating enemies. It is a tough concept to apply to ourselves because it requires us to see ways in which we and our enemies are the same. A good starting point is to look at what we have in common on a practical level, such as families, lifestyle, expectations, dreams, children. These links can be an introduction to later work on projection.

Skills   Visualisation. Physical expression. Observation.

Exercise 12.13   *Time: 20 min.*

Personal projection

Description   Individual work with paired feedback, looking at links between our enemies and ourselves.

Aims   To recognise aspects of ourselves that we often do not accept. To explore links between what we do not accept in ourselves and what our enemies represent.

Directions

1   Ask participants to draw up a list of things they dislike about themselves. Ask them to find things that they are genuinely uncomfortable about, or would really rather not acknowledge. They then add to the list things that they feel they are not, and would like to be. This list will not be shared with the whole group.   *5 min.*

2   In pairs, partners look at their lists, alongside the lists they made previously (in Exercise 12.12), stating three things they dislike about their enemy. Ask them to see how many links they can make between the two lists. What do their enemies have in common with themselves? Can they see in them anything they reject in themselves, or anything they would like to be and are not? Make sure that pairs spend time on the lists of both partners – five minutes each.   *10 min.*

Feedback and discussion   What links did participants find between what they do not accept about themselves and what their enemies represent? What does this tell them?   *5 min.*

Notes   Understanding how we project ourselves onto others can help us to confront our own fears and hates, and can be of value in facing projection thrown at us from others.

Skills   Self-awareness. Empathy.

Exercise 12.14 *Time: 10 min.*

OUTSIDERS

Description An interactive exercise exploring the effects of exclusive grouping on an individual.

Aims To explore how we react to experiences of rejection. To look at what it feels like to belong to a group.

Directions

1 Ask a volunteer to leave the room. The remainder of the group divide themselves into groups according to some agreed criterion – for example, hairstyle, eye colour, type of clothing, height or accent.   *3 min.*

2 The outsider is called in and guesses which group they belong to. They must state why they believe that group is their group. If the reason is wrong they may not join, even when they have picked the correct group.   *4 min.*

3 Continue with a new volunteer, giving as many participants as possible an opportunity to go outside, subject to time.

Feedback and discussion How do we behave when we do belong to a group? Is it easy to reject outsiders? Is it enjoyable? Do we empathise with the outsider or do we enjoy our power?   *3 min.*

Notes This exercise links with Exercise 3.18, but here the focus is on feelings and experiences of being rejected rather than communication. It can be used to focus a discussion about prejudice and how we react to belonging or not belonging. It could be developed into a study of personal experiences.

Skills Teamwork. Co-operation. Imagination. Trust.

Exercise 12.15 *Time: 60 min.*

FACING PROJECTION FROM OTHERS

Description Paired role-play exercise focused on facing anger and projection from others.

Aims To explore what underlies expressions of hatred and bigotry. To develop strategies for facing anger and projection from others with greater confidence.

Directions

1 Prepare POINTS OF VIEW cards (see page 106). Put participants in pairs and ask them to decide who is A and who is B. Give each pair one card. Partner A takes on the point of view and begins a conversation with B along those lines. B listens to what A has to say, and tries to find out what needs and fears lie at the root of it. A should take on the point of view with all their imagination, using every argument they have ever heard, and trying to get into the shoes of someone who really does hold that view. B should listen carefully, questioning and probing, and try to identify the real problem underneath what A is saying.   *10 min.*

2 Feedback in pairs. Did A feel that B was reaching something close to the truth? What questions were most revealing? What tactics were effective? How did each feel in their role?   *10 min.*

3 Pairs join up to form groups of four. Ask each group to draw up a set of guidelines (similar to the example at the end of this exercise) for use when facing someone else's projection, in the form of bigotry, prejudice, hate or aggression. What does the individual on the receiving end want to achieve? How do they react? What do they say? It will help participants to use their experience of stage 1, concentrating on how successful the questioning process was, and which tactics and approaches had effect.   *15 min.*

4 In the same groups, each group chooses a POINTS OF VIEW card to work on. Two members of the group take on the viewpoint. The other two work together, following their guidelines, to try to get to the root of the comments. Allow five minutes for preparation, five minutes for the role-play, five minutes for feedback within the groups.   *15 min.*

Feedback and discussion What guidelines could you use in your working environment? How could they influence your

POINTS OF VIEW

RACIST

They're taking all our homes and jobs. Why don't they just go back where they came from?

FANNING THE FLAMES
12.15

RACIST

There's a genetic difference between black and white, which explains why we are simply not equal.

FANNING THE FLAMES
12.15

SEXIST

Equal opportunities are all very well, but as soon as you give a woman a position of responsibility she leaves to have a baby.

FANNING THE FLAMES
12.15

ANTI-DISABLED

They make me feel awkward. I don't feel like eating. They shouldn't be allowed in restaurants if they can't feed themselves.

FANNING THE FLAMES
12.15

ANTI-GAY

They can do what they like in their own homes, but I'm not having them teach my children.

FANNING THE FLAMES
12.15

ANTI-UNEMPLOYED

They're all losers. There are plenty of jobs. They're just too lazy to go and look.

FANNING THE FLAMES
12.15

work? How can we find out whether the anger we are feeling towards someone includes projection? What guidelines could we employ in order to check ourselves?   *10 min.*

Notes   The sharing and feedback is important, and can give participants practical ideas to take away with them. It is important to find out if any participants found the contentious points of view upsetting. Their feelings can be shared with the group. In this way awareness of these issues is heightened.

This exercise is linked to Exercise 13.3, where the focus is on finding a response for one particular incident.

Skills   Active listening. Drawing out information. Empathy. Patience.

GUIDELINES ON FACING HATE, AGGRESSION OR PROJECTION

1   Allow the anger and emotion to come out. Don't try to arrest it.

2   In an outpouring there is little point in meeting the emotional point of view with facts. They will not be heard until the roots of the anger are addressed.

3   Listen carefully. Feed back what you are hearing and how you interpret it. For example: 'It seems to me that you're angry about the thought that black people get better housing than you.' This process could be developed into an exploration of the protagonist's insecurities, needs and fears.

4   Remember that reasoned argument will reach unhearing ears.

5   Acknowledge your own boundaries to yourself, such as how much insulting language you can take. Once you have established that you are not going to preach, you might be able to state what is acceptable and unacceptable to you without being felt to be judgmental.

6   Offer personal disclosure if and when appropriate, allowing the other individual to see you as a fallible human being with your own needs and fears.

STOKING THE FIRE

Inequalities and empowerment

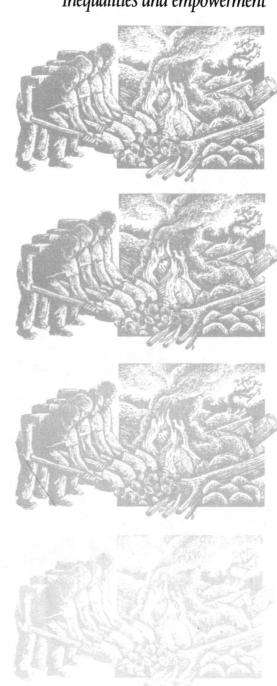

STOKING THE FIRE
Inequalities and empowerment

The flames have taken hold. They are burning with energy. The fuel is consumed as the flames grow higher. The stokers add fuel to the fire. It demands to be fed. The fuel burns quickly. The fire catches on huge logs, and takes hold with speed. Attempts to put the fire out meet with little success. The logs refuse to be extinguished, and there are many more ready to burn.

THE conflict is fuelled by arsonists, who delight in the fury of the flames. They are the stokers. The fuel is within their reach. The logs that are added to the fire are large and weighty. They are the logs of prejudice and oppression, and will not easily crumble or disintegrate. They cast shadows over our lives just as they stoke our fires. They burn with vigour and resist efforts to put them out.

There is still time for a mediator to enter the conflict and work on strategies for resolving it. But the work of the mediator will be tough. Social structures which engender injustice do not just disappear. The mediator needs a strategy not just to put out the near-blazing fire, but to bring about long-lasting change.

Focus Equal opportunities; unequal opportunities. Youth work as intervention between young people and injustice. Empowering young people.

Aims To tackle the exploitation that affects us and the young people we work with. To create an idea of what we would like our futures to be. To create a strategy for getting there. To explore ways of encouraging young people to take responsibility for their lives. To explore ways of encouraging young people to believe that they deserve choices and opportunities.

Key concepts Exploitation. Injustice, including social injustice. Patterns of behaviour. Empowerment.

Key questions What does social injustice mean in our lives and the lives of the young people we work with? What patterns of exploitation can you see in yourself and those around you? How can we encourage young people to believe that they deserve choice and opportunity? What does change mean in the context of our personal and working lives?

This section contains three two-and-a-half-hour sessions. Session 13 looks at personal experiences of injustice and strategies for immediate responses, and at what we need from our social environments. Session 14 deals with exploring patterns of behaviour and challenging destructive cycles. Session 15 focuses on unpacking motivations and reasons behind destructive actions, defining visions, and steps towards achieving them.

All training techniques (such as brainstorm, role-play and tableau work) are explained in TRAINING FOR TRAINERS.

Session 13

Introduction   Personal experience of social injustice; strategic responses to social injustice; and what we have a right to expect from our social environment.   *10 min.*

13.1 JACK AND JILL   *75 min.*
13.2 WHO DO YOU HURT?   *75 min.*
13.3 STRATEGIC RESPONSES   *30 min.*
13.4 COMMUNITY CARDS   *25 min.*

Reflection   *10 min.*

Notes   Exercises 13.1 and 13.2 are for single-sex groups, exploring the different experiences and responses of men and women. At the end of the exercise the two groups share their work and reflect on what they have seen. We recommend that you choose only one of these exercises and take *at least* the recommended 75 minutes. Exercise 13.3 explores strategic immediate responses to situations of prejudice. Exercise 13.4 closes the session with an exploration of what the participants expect from their community.

Exercise 13.1   *Time: 75 mins.*

JACK AND JILL

Description   A single-sex group writing exercise exploring the differences between growing up as a girl and growing up as a boy.

Aims   To enable women and men in the group to explore the different pressures put on them as they grew up. To explore how such pressures affect us and shape our perceptions.

Directions

1 Divide into two single-sex groups. Ask each group to create individual and group tableaux of the following stages of growing up: early childhood (baby to 5); first day at school; being a teenager; leaving home or taking first job; now; the future.   *15 min.*

2 Ask participants to discuss the similarities and differences within their group. What experiences are shared? What pressures and expectations, what pleasures and satisfactions, do they have in common?   *10 min.*

3 In the same groups, ask participants to respond to the following questions from their point of view as a woman or man, and, in writing, condense their responses into the story of a fictional girl or boy. This will be a collective story, with contributions from all the members of that group.

- As you grew up, what were you told that girls and boys should and should not do (for example, 'Big boys don't cry' or 'Girls can't climb trees')?
- What kinds of toys were you encouraged to play with?
- What pressures did you feel you had to submit to?
- What were the pressures on you as a teenage boy or girl?
- What expectations did others have of you?
- What did you think your future would be?
- What did you dream your future would be? What is the difference between what you thought and what you dreamt?   *30 min.*

4 Bring the two groups together. Ask each group to read out their story to the other. Both groups should then read out their stories a second time, but this time they change the personal pronouns so that 'she' becomes 'he', and 'her' becomes 'his', and *vice versa*. Those listening should try to get into the shoes of the fictional protagonist, and imagine what it must have felt like for them. *10 min.*

Feedback and discussion What surprised participants as they listened to the other group's story? What amused them? Why? How has it developed their understanding of another point of view? *10 min.*

Notes The pressures and expectations of girlhood and boyhood are very different, and it is not easy to imagine what it must have felt like to be in the other sex's shoes. The exercise addresses these points as an introduction to thinking about how anger, aggression and violence have affected us all differently. The next exercise uses further single-sex work to look at these areas in greater detail.

Skills Clear written expression. Listening with empathy. Co-operation.

WHO DO YOU HURT?

Description Single-sex group work using tableaux to look at experiences of and responses to anger, aggression and violence.

Aims To explore the different experiences of women and men in relation to anger and violence. To look at the different ways in which we can express our anger. To ask questions about the different expectations we have of women's and men's use of anger and aggression.

Directions

1 The two groups are going to work separately, preferably in different rooms, on tableaux to do with anger and aggression. Individually, within the single-sex groups, each person is asked for an immediate physical response – that is, in the form of a tableau or statue – to the words 'physical violence'. (They might, for example, hold up an arm to defend themselves against attack, or clench their fists in an aggressive pose.) Do not give the group any opportunity to think about their responses. Encourage them to respond immediately. *5 min.*

2 Ask for the same kind of physical responses to the following questions.
- What do women or men do when they feel angry?
- What do they do with their anger?
- How do you express your anger?
- How would you like to express your anger?
- How do women or men experience the anger of others?
- What do they do when they experience the anger of others? *5 min.*

3 Each group works towards producing collective tableaux representing the different views of its members. (You may find that some of the individual responses fit into categories or families and can be grouped together within the larger picture). Aim to create two such pictures, one for giving and one for receiving anger. *10 min.*

4 Divide each single-sex group into smaller groups. Ask participants to think of a moment in their life when their attitude, response, or reaction to physical violence changed. Each group chooses one person's experience to work on. Ask them to divide the story into three stages and show each stage

as a tableau. When the tableaux are ready, thoughts can be added to each of the characters at each stage. The aim here is to examine a turning point in someone's experience and find out what changed their attitude, how, and what effect that change has had on their lives.   *30 min.*

5   Bring the two single-sex groups together to share the work they have done so far. If they do not want to show their tableaux, they can talk about what they discovered. This sharing is an integral part of the exercise and should not be omitted.   *15 min.*

Feedback and discussion   What distinctive patterns did people see in the ways women and men have been encouraged and expected to handle anger? What different perceptions of anger did you observe – for example, violence as a response to social injustice versus violence as an expression of frustrated anger? What changes would participants like to see in the way we use aggression and teach others to use it? What surprises did they get from the exercise, and from dividing into single-sex groups? What did they gain from it? Would they like to work in single-sex groups again?   *10 min.*

Notes   This work should preferably be led by two trainers, one for each single-sex group. If it is not possible to have a female and a male worker at this stage, you will have to run the two groups alone. Give them the same instructions and send them off to do the work. Join the group of your own sex, by all means; but if possible give one member of the other group the role of facilitator and timekeeper, so that they can help in holding the group together. It is important that the groups remain single-sex – the trainer should not be an exception.

As the work begins with immediate physical responses to words, it is important to warm the group up first. Choose a warm-up game which will have the group moving round the room using their bodies.

Owing to a variety of social and cultural influences, women's and men's experiences of anger and aggression are often very different. This single-sex work is an opportunity to explore some of the differences.

Skills   Physical expression. Co-operation. Improvisation.

STRATEGIC RESPONSES

Description   Individual and paired work on finding a successful response to a particular provocation.

Aims   To practise anticipation of abusive language or gestures from others. To find a way of dealing with the abuse that is in keeping with the long-term aims of the person involved.

Directions

1   Introduce the exercise with an example – use the one given on page 115 or prepare your own. Explain that this exercise aims to anticipate the challenges we will face at work or at home and prepare us for a response.   *5 min.*

2   Ask each participant to think of a word, phrase or gesture that is used by others, whether in the workplace or at home, and about which they feel angry. Participants should ask themselves the following questions as preparation.
- What is it that angers me?
- Why do I want to change it or stop it?
- What does it tell me about the person involved?
- Am I on my own? What physical or moral support do I have?   *5 min.*

3   In pairs, ask partners to work on a strategic response for both of their examples, following these three simple guidelines: (1) define what the word, phrase or gesture means; (2) say who it applies to; (3) say what it means when used abusively.   *10 min.*

4   In the whole group, share some of the examples that individuals have been working on. It is good to hear everyone's ideas, but if you have a large group this may not be possible. You could ask for examples which people think may be relevant to others.   *5 min.*

Feedback and discussion   What is the effect of having a strategic response? How will participants use it?   *5 min.*

Notes   Having a strategic response at our fingertips is like having a magic nugget in our hands. When we use it we know that we are respecting ourselves and our ideals. It builds our self-esteem.

Skills Acknowledging emotions and difficulties. Preparing an argument and following it through.

STRATEGIC RESPONSES: AN EXAMPLE

A YOUNG man in a school was always swearing. A member of staff found some of his language offensive, in particular the word 'cunt'.

She decided to approach him, and the next time he used the word she asked·him if he knew what it meant. She explained that it is part of a woman's sexual organs, otherwise called a vagina. She elaborated on the fact that every woman has one. She asked if he would ever call his mother a cunt. He would not. She reminded him that his mother has a cunt, as does his grand-mother and his sisters, and that every time he used the word abusively he was abusing them as well.

She repeated the facts. A cunt is a woman's vagina. All women have one. When its name is used as a term of abuse it abuses every woman, including the women he would never want to insult in that way.

The young man was taken aback by her calm, unashamed use of the words 'cunt' and 'vagina', and by the links she made between the word and his mother. The woman felt liberated by her stance. She no longer had to allow pupils to use abusive language that she found so offensive. She no longer had to compromise her feelings.

COMMUNITY CARDS

Description Small-group discussion, using stimulus cards, on what we can expect from our working environments.

Aims To explore what we deserve from our working environments, what we actually have, and what we need.

Directions

1 Divide into small groups and give a COMMUNITY CARD (see page 116) to each group. Ask participants to discuss the quotation, thinking of their working environment as their community. What do we have a right to expect from this community? What is the reality of our situation?   *5 min.*

2 In the same small groups, participants decide on three words describing what they expect or need from their environment, and a sentence which sums up what the reality is for them. If members of the group have different views about this, they should decide on two sentences which summarise their thoughts – but no more than two.   *10 min.*

3 Participants come together and hear feedback from each of the small groups. This should not take long – each group is feeding back just three words and one or two sentences. *5 min.*

Feedback and discussion Is there a disparity between what we *should* have from our community and what we *do* have? If your community is not sustaining you, then what is? Where does your support and encouragement come from?   *5 min.*

Notes The exercise focuses on what we think we deserve from work and what our working environment could be. This kind of work is a vital part of working towards a future that we want. The group could look at other aspects of community – for example, with friends and with family.

Skills Uncovering and expressing needs. Group listening.

COMMUNITY CARDS

COMMUNITY CARD

'There is a significant gap between what we have a right to expect of our community – intimacy, trust, mutual commitment and support, an environment that sustains us all – and what the reality has become. Something is missing from our experience of ourselves as a community.'

STOKING THE FIRE
13.4

COMMUNITY CARD

'There is a significant gap between what we have a right to expect of our community – intimacy, trust, mutual commitment and support, an environment that sustains us all – and what the reality has become. Something is missing from our experience of ourselves as a community.'

STOKING THE FIRE
13.4

COMMUNITY CARD

'There is a significant gap between what we have a right to expect of our community – intimacy, trust, mutual commitment and support, an environment that sustains us all – and what the reality has become. Something is missing from our experience of ourselves as a community.'

STOKING THE FIRE
13.4

COMMUNITY CARD

'There is a significant gap between what we have a right to expect of our community – intimacy, trust, mutual commitment and support, an environment that sustains us all – and what the reality has become. Something is missing from our experience of ourselves as a community.'

STOKING THE FIRE
13.4

COMMUNITY CARD

'There is a significant gap between what we have a right to expect of our community – intimacy, trust, mutual commitment and support, an environment that sustains us all – and what the reality has become. Something is missing from our experience of ourselves as a community.'

STOKING THE FIRE
13.4

COMMUNITY CARD

'There is a significant gap between what we have a right to expect of our community – intimacy, trust, mutual commitment and support, an environment that sustains us all – and what the reality has become. Something is missing from our experience of ourselves as a community.'

STOKING THE FIRE
13.4

Session 14

Introduction

Exploring patterns of behaviour; challenging destructive patterns. *10 min.*

Reflection *10 min.*

Notes Exercise 14.5 is an introduction to the themes of the session. Exercise 14.6 explores power relationships by looking at the behaviour of the persecutor, the victim and the rescuer. Exercise 14.7 explores through role-play the interaction between these three types of behaviour and how to change them into more constructive modes of behaviour. Exercise 14.8 prepares participants for the next session. If extra time is needed for Exercie 14.7, then Exercise 14.8 could be done by participants at home and brought to the next session.

Exercise 14.5 *Time: 30 min.*

DESCRIBING A HABIT

Description An exercise in which individuals define and confront a habit that they find difficult to change.

Aims To understand the nature of our habits and determine ways of tackling them.

Directions

1 Participants can work individually or in pairs. Ask them all to identify a personal habit that they find extremely difficult to change, such as smoking, or eating a chocolate after every meal. *3 min.*

2 Ask participants to write down, or describe to their partners, an experience involving their habit – perhaps some occasion when the strength of the habit led them to behave anti-socially or to break some rule. They should describe all the feelings they had, as well as what they said and what they did.

Ask them to list all their thoughts at the time, in the order in which they occurred, and number them 1 to 10. Do they see a natural progression in these thoughts? Were they simply trying to rationalise – find pretexts for – whatever action they were about to take? How did they go about this? *10 min.*

3 Are there any alternative thoughts they could have had? Ask participants to imagine what they might be. It is important to recognise how our behaviour is supported by thought processes. If we can find ways of changing the thought process underlying a habit, then the behaviour might possibly change with it. *5 min.*

4 Participants can share some of their descriptions of their habits and the things they do to support them. *5 min.*

Feedback and discussion Does targeting the habit in this way help us to understand our behaviour a little better? How can this understanding make it easier to work out possible strategies for change? Who is in control, the habit or you? *7 min.*

Notes You can imagine applying this exercise to really tough subject matter: for example, using it with someone who is always getting into fights; with someone who habitually destroys relationships and friendships; with someone who finds it difficult to hold down a job; with someone who finds it impossible to control their anger.

In this exercise the individual does the work. There is no analyst – only the individual identifying their own behaviour, spotting trends, and devising positive strategies for change. But it is good for members to help each other through this process. The sharing of information can be mutually informative. This work is developed in Exercise 17.3.

Skills Self-awareness. Clarity. Expression. Analysis.

PAM, REGGIE AND VERNON

Description Exploration in small groups of some of the behaviour shown by persecutor, victim and rescuer.

Aims To explore the type of behaviour which maintains unequal power relationships. To identify personal experiences of the roles within a 'power game'.

Directions

1 Share the information sheet THE POWER GAME TRIANGLE with the group (see page 120). *9 min.*

2 Divide into small groups, giving each group one of the three PROFILE CARDS (see page 121). Ask them to fill it out, giving two items under each heading. The idea is to build a caricature of each type – persecutor, victim and rescuer. *5 min.*

3 Each group chooses one of their phrases, a tone of voice and a body stance to go with it. In the case of Pam Persecutor, for example, the phrase might be 'Don't ever speak to me like that again'; the tone of voice might be loud and sharp; and the stance might be standing up and pointing a finger. Each group practises enacting this behaviour. They should aim to present their character to the other groups by speaking and acting in unison. Rather than exploring individual interpretations of the role, the group works to find a collective identity using the agreed phrase, tone of voice and body stance. *3 min.*

4 The groups now present themselves to each other in role. Maintaining their group identity as either persecutor, victim or rescuer, all the groups move around the room exploring the ways in which they interact with each other. At this point the groups may want to use different phrases or even develop a conversation.

If there are more than three groups you will get the opportunity to see what happens when, for example, two victim groups meet. *8 min.*

Feedback and discussion How did participants feel in the roles they were playing? Which of the roles is most familiar to them? Who else do they know who often seems to be playing one of these roles? Can they think of current situations in which they themselves are playing one of these roles? *5 min.*

Notes We use the terms 'persecutor', 'rescuer' and 'victim' to signify behaviours, not people. There will be aspects of each role that we are familiar with, either in ourselves or in others. In conversation an individual could shift from one role to another, or play aspects of all three. But the maintenance of this particular power triangle relies on the participation of all three roles. Each of the roles has its pay-offs, which is why participation in the triangle continues. When we use the word 'victim' we refer to a role, not to someone who is a genuine victim of oppression. A genuine victim needs real support and help and will welcome possibilities of change. On the other hand, those who are in the victim role typically reject possible change. For example, they might respond to every possibility offered, 'Yes but . . .'

This exercise is an introduction to THE POWER GAME, which follows.

Skills Physical expression. Observation. Exploration.

THE POWER GAME

Description Role-play game in threes looking at the power dynamics in a three-way relationship.

Aims To explore the behaviour of the persecutor, the victim and the rescuer. To explore our own feelings when playing each of those roles. To look at ways of changing the roles.

Directions

1 Ask participants to spend a few minutes individually thinking of a time when they have been in the persecutor role, the rescuer role and the victim role. What did their behaviour involve? What kind of language did they use? Refer to all observations made in Exercise 14.6. *5 min.*

2 In groups of three, ask participants to draw an imaginary triangle on the floor which corresponds to the power game triangle (see page 120). One person stands in each position. Each person can play either an adult or a child, but there must be at least one of each in the group. Each participant keeps their character throughout the exercise. *1 min.*

3 Begin the first round with a discussion. For example, a family might be engaged in an argument about where to go on holiday; or a parent and child and the child's teacher might be discussing the child's progress.

Participants play the role of persecutor, rescuer or victim, according to their position in the triangle. Allow three minutes only. *3 min.*

4 Allow one minute for participants to jot down feelings and thoughts about their role. *1 min.*

5 Each participant moves round one place on the triangle, and therefore changes the role they are playing. But everyone keeps their character. So, someone playing a parent and a persecutor in the first round would become a rescuer but maintain the character of a parent. Participants should move round the triangle physically, so that they actually walk towards the their next role. Participants continue the discussion in their new roles, again for three minutes. *3 min.*

6 Again, allow one minute for participants to jot down feelings and thoughts about their role. *1 min.*

THE POWER GAME TRIANGLE

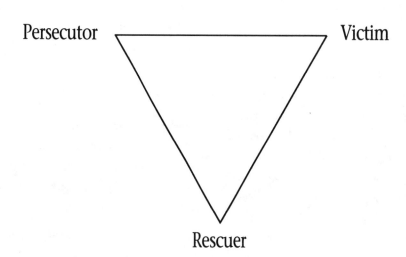

Persecutor   Victim

Rescuer

Persecutor
Bully

Says: *You won't . . .You mustn't . . . You will . . . You must . . . It's your fault.* Uses imperatives and orders. Language full of blame and threat. Presumes that the victim is always wrong and needs to be corrected.

Pay-offs: Often get what they want in the short term.

Drawbacks: No basis for respect from others. Often unsatisfactory relationships with people.

Needs within the role: To feel important and powerful.

Rescuer
Do-gooder

Says: *You can't . . . Poor you . . . You shouldn't have to . . . You need my help.* Uses placatory words. Language full of put-downs towards the victim and admonitions towards the persecutor. Presumes that the victim is inadequate and incapable of self-help.

Pay-offs: Manipulative power and control.

Drawbacks: Insecurity of falling between two camps. Often afraid of losing friends.

Needs within the role: To be liked by everyone. To be indispensable to the lives of others.

Victim
Door-mat

Says: *I can't . . . I'll fail . . . I don't know how . . . It's my fault.* Uses negatives and denials. Language full of dismissals and self-pity. Assumes inability to succeed or change.

Pay-offs: Others take responsibility. No high expectations to live up to.

Drawbacks: Low self-esteem. Powerlessness.

Needs within the role: To be looked after and to be cared for.

PROFILE CARDS

Pam/Pete Persecutor

Typical phrases:

Tone of voice:

How she/he stands, sits, walks:

STOKING THE FIRE
14.6B

Reggie/Regina Rescuer

Typical phrases:

Tone of voice:

How she/he stands, sits, walks:

STOKING THE FIRE
14.6B

Vera/Vernon Victim

Typical phrases:

Tone of voice:

How she/he stands, sits, walks:

STOKING THE FIRE
14.6B

7 Participants move on to the next position exactly as before, keeping their character but changing their role, and continue the discussion for a further three minutes.   *3 min.*

8 One minute for reflection on the new role.   *1 min.*

9 Share the information sheet THE TRIANGLE OF CHANGE (page 123). Discuss how the roles differ from those in the power game. How might the interaction between the characters change?   *10 min.*

10 In the same groups of three, with the same characters, again take up positions on the triangle. This time the role of the rescuer is replaced by that of the mediator, whose aim is to transform the roles of victim and persecutor into those of disputing parties. Spend ten minutes with one person in the role of the mediator. The task of those playing the persecutor and the victim is, with the help of the mediator, to change their roles into those of disputing parties.

Allow two minutes for participants to note down any differences exerienced as a result of the one changed role. (We recommend that extra time be allowed if all three are to take on the role of mediator. Twelve minutes will be sufficient time for only one person to take on this role.)   *12 min.*

Feedback and discussion   What were the possibilities of changing the power dynamics in the role-play? In triangular situations at work, what could participants do to change the dynamics? What have they gained from this exercise?   *5 min.*

Notes   Often in a power game, it is only one player who decides to change the situation. That individual can transform the whole game. Just as the rescuer can become a mediator, so the persecutor or the victim can put themselves in a position where they can see the dispute as an opportunity for both teaching *and* learning. Where such change occurs, you no longer have people interfering and instructing each other; you have people *interacting*. It is no longer a power game.

This work could be focused to look at individual experiences of being in one of the three power-game roles, and what it would take to transform it – that is, what verbal language, gestures and body language could turn the role into something more constructive.

Though opposed in certain obvious ways, victim and persecutor can have much in common. Victims do not like being victims and may turn on a rescuer, blaming them for not having done something well enough, thus placing themselves in the persecutor position and making the rescuer a victim. For example:

YOUNG PERSON (VICTIM). What am I going to do? I've got no money and I was sacked from my job last week.
YOUTH WORKER (RESCUER). I'll ring up your ex-employers and see what I can do.
          [*Ex-employers will not change their decision*
YOUNG PERSON (PERSECUTOR). Sod you. Think you can help, but you don't do a thing. You're useless.

Skills   Improvisation. Role-play. Interaction. Expression.

THE TRIANGLE OF CHANGE

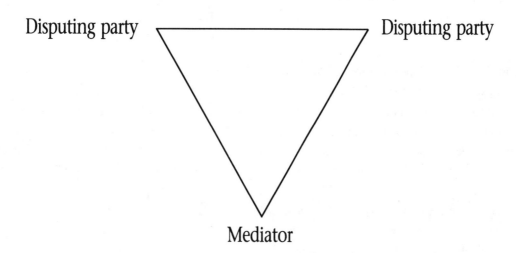

Disputing party   Disputing party

Mediator

The mediator

The mediator has no interest in maintaining the difficulties. They are on neither the persecutor's nor the victim's side. They are neutral. They are there to help the others resolve their own difficulties. They are not trying to make friends, and they are not merely trying to pacify. They are trying to find the causes of the conflict, and the feelings which need to be expressed. They aim to uncover the common ground on which agreement can be built.

Key skills   Careful, active listening; drawing out underlying issues, needs and fears; impartiality.

Disputing parties

The roles of the persecutor and the victim become interchangeable. The mediator has encouraged them to look at the difficulties in their relationship and what their needs are instead of focusing on who is to blame. Once the focus has been changed there is room for exchange of feelings between the two disputants. Both are now in a position to give and receive personal information and support.

The triangle of change

The people involved may still have disagreements and conflicts, but through a mediator they have an opportunity to resolve the problem in a way that meets everyone's needs. By changing your view of your own role (whether it is persecutor, victim or rescuer), and changing your perspective of the problem, you change the dynamics of the power game and make movement possible.

Exercise 14.8 *Time: 25 min.*

MY VISION

Description A paired exercise to establish what participants would like their work to be.

Aims To regenerate goals and aims within work.

Directions

1 The exercise is based around these questions: (1) When you walk into the workplace (perhaps the youth club) at the beginning of a session, what do you see and feel and what do you want to see and feel? (2) While you are at work, what do you do, see and feel and what do you want to do, see and feel? (3) When you leave, what do you feel and what do you want to feel?

Divide into pairs. A asks B the first question; B answers. A helps B to visualise what they really want to see, and to imagine what they really want to feel. They should aim to distil these things into one sentence before swapping over. Spend the same length of time on A's vision before moving to the next question.   *5 min.*

2 A asks B the second question. Using the format outlined above, they should end up with one sentence to sum up B's response. Swap and allow the same time for B to ask A the question.   *5 min.*

3 A asks B the third question. Using the same format, they should end up with one sentence to sum up B's response. Swap and allow the same time for B to ask A the question.
     5 min.

4 Feedback in the whole group. Each participant should have three sentences to read out.   *5 min.*

Feedback and discussion What prevents you achieving your vision? What can you do about it?   *5 min.*

Notes Focus on visions and aspirations which offer a practical ideal to work towards. If time proves too short, ask participants to have their answers ready for the next session. This exercise is an introduction to Exercise 15.10 and needs to be done beforehand, either in the group or as homework.

Skills Listening. Encouraging. Imagination.

Session 15

Introduction Identifying motives and reasons behind destructive action. Defining visions and steps towards achieving them.   *10 min.*

15.9	THROWING THE STONE	*65 min.*
15.10	FROM PRESENT TO FUTURE	*65 min.*

Reflection   *10 min.*

Notes Exercise 15.9 uses role-play to reconstruct the causes and circumstances of an imaginary event, and attempts to unpack the motives underlying it. Exercise 15.10 explores our visions of the future and strategies for realising them.

Exercise 15.9 *Time: 65 min.*

THROWING THE STONE

Description A role-play exercise exploring the possible reasons behind a violent incident.

Aims To uncover the causal sequence behind a seemingly random act of violence. To explore the motives behind the act. To look for alternatives to violent behaviour.

Directions

1 Divide into groups of about six or seven. Each group will create and act out a story. Both stories end with the same picture: a person holding a stone and about to throw it at a window. All the groups create the story by answering these questions about that picture:

• Is there any significance in the stone-thrower's choice of this particular window?

• Is the person alone? If not, who are they with?

• If others are present, are they involved in any way?

• What was the final straw that led to the decision to break the window?

• Where did that take place?

• What led up to that? Who else was involved?

• What incidents helped to create the feelings and frustrations behind the incident? *10 min.*

2 Ask groups to recap the basics of the story, divide up the roles, and prepare the scenes, ending with a frozen picture of a stone about to be thrown. *10 min.*

3 The groups act out their scenes for each other. Ask for feedback from the audience about what they perceive is actually going on. What is at the root? The role-play might end, for example, with a child throwing a stone through a school staff-room window, and we might have been shown scenes which tell us that she was falsely accused of stealing and suspended from school for a week. So, at the root of the incident lie intense personal feelings of injustice, isolation, not being listened to, not being believed, feelings of inadequacy and anger. *10 min.*

4 In the same groups, ask participants to think about ways of addressing the roots of the incident, focusing on whether there is a pattern of behaviour and, if there is, how it could be

changed. Below are some useful questions to consider. You could use these in discussion with a group once they have come up with their own ideas.

Finding a pattern of behaviour Has a similar incident happened before? Is it likely to happen again?

Changing a pattern of behaviour What outside forces could prevent it from happening again? What could the stone-thrower do to stop responding in the same way? What are possible alternative responses? What would be helpful responses from friends and onlookers? *15 min.*

5 Participants come together to share these ideas and develop them into a checklist. *10 min.*

Feedback and discussion Participants might consider the following questions. Do you understand why the stone is being thrown? Do you have any sympathy with the perpetrator? What is the difference between understanding and sympathising? Can you recognise any destructive patterns in your own life? *10 min.*

Notes This exercise can be useful with a young person who is aware of destructive cycles and wants to change them. If there has been a violent incident, in a youth club, for instance, this exercise could be used to find out what people thought about it. Use the structure, but end the scene freezing on the incident you want to focus on. Adapt the questions to make them relevant. Refer to Exercises 9.12 and 9.13 for ideas on a questioning process for tableau work.

When this exercise is done with young people, the questions will raise real issues for them and bring out deeply felt responses. You can use the exercise to find out what young people are experiencing in relation to these questions, without directly questioning them about their personal lives.

Skills Imaginative story-building. Group listening and idea-building. Accepting other people's ideas and enacting them.

Exercise 15.10   *Time: 65 min.*

FROM PRESENT TO FUTURE

Description   Group tableau work to devise a strategy for improving participants' working environments.

Aims   To clarify aims and objectives within our working environments. To find ways of achieving them.

Directions

1   Divide participants into groups of four or five. Ask each group to create two pairs of tableaux on the theme of their working environment. One pair of tableaux will represent *What we see* and *What we'd like to see*; the other will represent *How we feel about it* and *How we'd like to feel about it*. Ask groups to look for elements of the workplace that they can all relate to. If they find it impossible to accommodate their different viewpoints within collective tableaux, they can create more than one tableau under each heading.   *25 min.*

2   Ask groups to share their tableaux with the whole group. Check what is going on in each picture. Divide a large sheet of paper into three columns headed (from left to right) PRESENT, PROCESS and FUTURE. Under the heading PRESENT, write down what you observe to be happening in the *What we see* and *What we feel* tableaux. Under the heading FUTURE, write down what you observe to be happening in the *What we'd like to see* and *What we'd like to feel* tableaux. The PROCESS column will be used for looking at how to get from the present to the future.   *15 min.*

3   You now have several experiences and ideals under the PRESENT and FUTURE headings. Choose one example to work with. First recap and clarify what is desired for the future, and make sure that what is written under the FUTURE heading is accurate. Pose the following questions one at a time. (1) How will we know when we've got there? Write the answers under the FUTURE heading. (2) How do we work towards achieving this? Write the answers under PROCESS. (3) What is the first thing I will do about it when I get to work tomorrow? Write the answers under the PROCESS heading.   *15 min.*

Feedback and discussion   What did you gain from this? How could you use it elsewhere? What is the most difficult step for you to take in the whole process?   *10 min.*

Notes   This exercise develops the work begun in Exercise 14.8. It is useful work to do with a staff team. It enables a team to pin down where the difficulties lie, and look at how the first step to changing the situation can be taken. It can also be adapted for use with young people to assess how they can go about achieving what they want. If a group has difficulty identifying the ways in which the present situation can be addressed, encourage participants to consider the specific incidents or conditions which caused it. The PROCESS column will then show the responses to these specifics.

The basis of this work is that effective change can always begin with your immediate social environment – so, if a young person is angry about the injustice they face in the wider social environment (with racism, job prospects, homelessness, or whatever) they can begin addressing it by working on making their immediate environment (their youth club, for instance) what they want it to be.

Skills   Imagination. Physical expression. Teamwork. Planning.

THE BLAZE

Crisis management, recovery and reparation

THE BLAZE
Crisis management, recovery and reparation

There is no shortage of logs to bring up the blaze. The flames leap and the fire rages. The logs are consumed by the flames. The huge blaze burns and it consumes all it touches. But it can also be a force for regeneration, a catalyst for new growth. The conflict blazes. There is damage and pain. Some are burnt by the fire; some are standing well clear of it. But no-one is untouched by the blazing conflict.

ONCE a fire is in full blaze the options are limited – we run away from it, or try to put it out, or run into it. The third option looks suicidal, but there are those who walk into flames confident that they will be unharmed. We can take on the role of fire-fighter, dress ourselves in flame-resistant clothing, enter the fire and remain unscathed. Mediators may enter blazing conflicts, and although they may be affected by what happens they should not be harmed. This third option is not about putting the fire out; it is about showing the way out of it to those who are in the middle. When we are in the middle of a blaze, the smoke and fumes overcome us, and the exit route may not be clear. Mediators can lead the way to the escape route for those who want to take it. What will make us flame-proof? Can we remain neutral? Do we have vested interests which will compromise us? What are the exits that we offer those in the blaze?

Focus Coping in a crisis. Recovery from a crisis. Analysis of what is going on in a crisis, and what is at the root of it.

Aims To explore what is going on in situations of crisis. To examine the behaviour which lies at the root of it. To identify and change recurring patterns of destructive behaviour. To explore personal and professional needs and resources in a crisis. To explore strategies for recovery from a crisis situation.

Key concepts Thought patterns. Facts and interpretations. Crisis and change. Recovery and reparation.

Key questions What goes on in a crisis situation? What lies at the roots of destructive behaviour? What approaches could we use to change recurring patterns of behaviour? What do we need to survive and recover from crisis?

This section contains three two-and-a-half-hour sessions. Session 16 looks at getting to the roots of a specific crisis situation, exploring strategies for dealing with each different root, and the creation of a 'fire drill' as a strategy for group management of a crisis. Session 17 explores destructive patterns of behaviour, and the development of individual strategies for personal intervention and of methods for handling mistakes and failures. Session 18 focuses on exploring the various methods available for reparation and recovery, developing staff strategies for recovery from crisis situations, and developing negotiation skills.

All training techniques (such as brainstorm, role-play and tableau work) are explained in TRAINING FOR TRAINERS.

Session 16

Exercise 16.1 *Time: 70 min.*

WHAT'S GOING ON?

Introduction Getting to the roots of a specific crisis situation and exploring strategies for dealing with each different root. Creation of a 'fire drill' as a strategy for group management of a crisis. *10 min.*

16.1 WHAT'S GOING ON?	*70 min.*
16.2 FIRE DRILL	*60 min.*

Reflection *10 min.*

Notes Exercise 16.1 explores what is at the root of situations of intense conflict and focuses on areas of potential change. Exercise 16.2 works towards the creation of an emergency procedure for a whole staff group as well as individual members to use in times of crisis.

Description A large-group exercise which explores what is at the root of situations of intense conflict and focuses on areas of potential change.

Aims To develop a set of strategies to get to the roots of difficult conflicts. To distinguish the various layers that exist in any situation involving extreme violence or anger. To develop appropriate techniques for responding to each of these layers.

Directions

1 Take an actual, current situation of conflict to work on or use an imagined situation as your example. One possible such situation could be set in the education department of a male prison: the teaching staff have requested a training workshop to look at new ways of dealing with the anger and aggression of the inmates in the classroom. In the following directions it is assumed that you are using this example as your context, though the exercise can easily be applied to any situation of conflict.

2 Begin with a brainstorm session. Ask the group to give their first responses to the words 'teacher' or 'tutor', then 'student' or 'pupil', and finally 'education' or 'learning'. Ask them to respond to these words from their own perspective and then, once they have completed all three, to give the type of responses they would imagine those on the other side of the conflict (in this case the inmates) would have to these three words. Responses could be written up in two columns to make comparisons between the two lists easier. Point out the gaps or similarities between the two lists. *20 min.*

3 Put some questions to the whole group: What's going on? What's going on that's visible? What do you see? What do you feel during a session? How do you react? Ask for responses which focus on the physical, the immediate. Typical responses here would be: fidgeting, noise, verbal abuse, no learning taking place, feeling intimidated, lots of anger. Another way of expressing the above questions would be to ask: What are the blocks to teaching and learning that exist between you and them, between them and you, and finally among themselves? It might be useful to refer to the brainstorm list.

4 Ask the group to imagine that the things they described in stage 3 are only the very top of a large pyramid. Hand out copies of the pyramid diagram (see page 133), and ask participants to write those things (or a selection of them) in the top right-hand section (that is, at the top of the CONFLICT column). (Trainers can refer to the example of a filled-in pyramid on page 132.)

This is the area of crisis management. The tutors (in this case) need immediate and effective strategies to cope with crises when they occur. This is how to ensure the safety of all those involved. Key questions are: How to cope? What tools do we need? Participants can make their own suggestions here, but what we need essentially is a fire drill – an emergency procedure for staff groups as well as individuals in crisis situations. (Exercise 16.2 develops such a drill.) This work should be considered as damage limitation, and is an appropriate response to conflict at this level. If we wish to become involved in preventive work, we need to examine one layer deeper.

5 The key question as we move down to the next layer of the pyramid is: What feeds all the things we see and feel in the top section? What lies immediately beneath them? Typical answers would be: insecurity, feeling threatened, lack of trust, suspicion.

Ask participants to write down their responses in the middle section of the right-hand CONFLICT column of the pyramid.   *20 min.*

6 The parallel question to explore is: What do we need to change all these things that are blocking the process of learning and development? What is missing? How do we create it? Typical responses could be: trust, rules and boundaries, agreements, affirming behaviour, mutual respect, non-threatening atmosphere. These responses can be written in the middle section of the left-hand CHANGE column of the pyramid.

At this level we are involved in preventive and curative work. The more work we do at this level, the greater is the possibility that we can handle or defuse crises if and when they occur. (The first five sections of this manual are full of suggestions for exercises that can help create some of the

conditions listed above. See, for example, Exercises 2.10, 6.13, 8.10, 11.9.) But we are aware that there are still many unexamined stones supporting this middle layer of the pyramid. There are still cycles and patterns of behaviour which make the building of trust, for example, impossible unless they are addressed and confronted. We need to venture one stage deeper.

7 The questioning process continues, this time focusing on the bottom level of the pyramid. What happens when you try to build trust? What happens when you challenge the group? What patterns of behaviour are sustaining all the things listed at stage 5? What are those things rooted in? What patterns of behaviour can you identify in your classroom? When you challenge the behaviour, what are you interfering with? How are the students intrepreting their present situation, and how do their interpretations depend on past experiences? In the context of the prison class, responses could be: victims, others to blame, justifications, past experiences, reflex responses. Write down any responses in the right-hand CONFLICT column of the pyramid.   *20 min.*

8 The key parallel question is: What can we do to change the obstructive patterns of behaviour? What needs to take place if everyone is to regain control of their own actions? In the lower section of the left-hand CHANGE column of the pyramid you can list some of the exercises from Session 17, which is entirely devoted to patterns of behaviour. These patterns are the foundation stones of the whole pyramid. Changes at this level will have a profound effect on any situation of conflict. If we address only the top two sections of the pyramid the effects will be more limited, although in the short term this may be beneficial and helpful.

Feedback and discussion In what ways has the pyramid scheme helped participants to see the layers that exist in the specific area of conflict that they chose to explore? What different strategies will they need for dealing with each layer? At what level of the pyramid do they think they deal with their own conflicts? Is there potential for further development? What do participants need in order to explore their work in greater depth?   *10 min.*

Notes The pyramid offers a sound schematic picture of the structure of conflict, and clarifies how the job of confronting conflict is a matter of addressng the situation layer by layer, and finally reaching what lies at the foundation. Exercise 10.4 offers a good example of how this pyramid can operate. All three layers need careful consideration, but it is only as you approach the base of the pyramid that you are really getting to the core of the conflict, to the very centre of all the people involved. It is only by tackling this layer that you can bring about fundamental change in situations of deep and recurring conflict.

Skills Exploration. Analysis. Recall. Observation. Planning. Communication.

Example 16.1

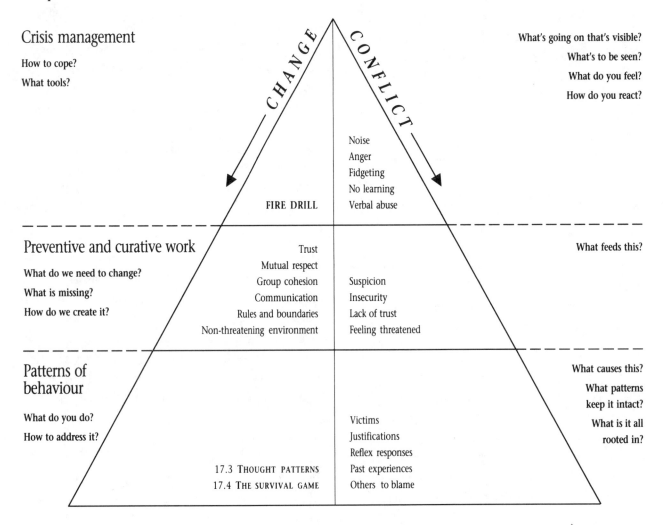

Crisis management

How to cope?
What tools?

CHANGE CONFLICT

What's going on that's visible?
What's to be seen?
What do you feel?
How do you react?

Noise
Anger
Fidgeting
No learning
Verbal abuse

FIRE DRILL

Preventive and curative work

What do we need to change?
What is missing?
How do we create it?

Trust
Mutual respect
Group cohesion
Communication
Rules and boundaries
Non-threatening environment

Suspicion
Insecurity
Lack of trust
Feeling threatened

What feeds this?

Patterns of behaviour

What do you do?
How to address it?

17.3 THOUGHT PATTERNS
17.4 THE SURVIVAL GAME

Victims
Justifications
Reflex responses
Past experiences
Others to blame

What causes this?
What patterns keep it intact?
What is it all rooted in?

WHAT'S GOING ON?

Crisis management

What's going on that's visible?

What's to be seen?

What do you feel?

How do you react?

How to cope?

What tools?

CONFLICT

CHANGE

Preventive and curative work

What feeds this?

What do we need to change?

What is missing?

How do we create it?

Patterns of behaviour

What causes this?

What patterns keep it intact?

What is it all rooted in?

What do you do?

How to address it?

Exercise 16.2 *Time: 60 min.*

FIRE DRILL

Description An exercise in small and large groups which works towards the creation of an emergency procedure for a staff group as well as for individuals to use in times of crisis.

Aims To highlight the needs and fears of the staff in terms of personal safety. To determine the boundaries of responsibility and the expectations of management and staff. To work out a safety procedure for the benefit of staff as well as young people. To work out ways in which this procedure could be implemented and supported. To explore needs in relation to staff training.

Directions

1 Ask every member of the group to identify two fears they have in the work environment, especially in relation to situations that could get out of hand, and two needs they would have if their fears were to be realised.   *5 min.*

2 Participants now read out their fears in turn, then their needs. Draw any common needs and fears together while they are being read. For example: 'My fear is that I will lose control and make the situation worse' and 'My need is for other people to take over if I seem to be losing control' (facilitators could write these up for the group). At the end of the sharing, with the help of the group, try to synthesise all the needs and fears into as few words as possible.   *5 min.*

3 In small groups, ask members to share their thoughts on what they consider to be their boundaries of responsibility. Do female and male participants have similar responsibilities in times of crisis? Is the intervention of a male or female more appropriate in certain circumstances? Where do they feel their responsibilities should end? When does safety become paramount? Do the expectations of management coincide with these boundaries? The idea is to work towards identifying the moment at which the staff will push their 'fire alarm button'.   *10 min.*

4 Each small group now agrees and feeds back a short report.   *5 min.*

5 Reflecting back on Exercises 8.9 and 8.10, as well as all the information gathered in stages 1 and 3 of the present exercise,

the group should now start work on an emergency fire drill. There should be consensus about the point at which they would push the alarm button. This is vital for the confidence of every individual, as well as the efficient implementation of the measures. In a large group, members should list the order of events.

Under each event, relevant details should be worked out: When does it happen? Who decides? Who does what? Who supports whom? Specific responsibilities? What specific support is needed? Are there any back-up procedures if things go wrong? When would outside help be called for?   *15 min.*

6 Once the overall strategy has been worked out, small working groups should be formed. Every group should be asked to explore a certain stage in the proceedings. For example, one group might work on the question of who should intervene in a crisis situation. How do you decide which staff are the most appropriate? In formulating their strategy, participants should of course draw on their own experiences of effective and ineffective intervention.   *10 min.*

7 Groups feed back short reports to the whole group.   *5 min.*

Feedback and discussion What further work needs to be done? What action still needs to be taken? What staff training will this entail? Do participants feel safer and more secure for having gone through this process? Have they found any other value in the process?   *5 min.*

Notes The drill could be ordered in various ways. One way would be to have the stages defined in one column, the specific action to be taken in another, the specific person in another, and in the last column any supportive action that would be taking place at each stage. Participants could use simulated situations to practise tactics, to gain clarity about procedures, to gain confidence. In the workplace, it is a good idea to involve young people in this kind of preparation and rehearsal. The drill is more likely to work – and less likely ever to be needed – if everyone has a share of the responsibility for it.

Skills Teamwork. Support. Observation. Communication. Negotiation. Training. Planning. Clarity.

Session 17

Introduction Exploring destructive patterns of behaviour and developing individual strategies for personal intervention. Devising methods for handling mistakes and failures. *10 min.*

17.3 THOUGHT PATTERNS   *45 min.*
17.4 THE SURVIVAL GAME   *45 min.*
17.5 SUPPORT YOURSELF   *40 min.*

Reflection   *10 min.*

Notes Exercise 17.3 is an individual written exercise exploring thought patterns at moments of particular stress or difficulty. Exercise 17.4 is an individual and interactive exercise exploring how our interpretations of past events influence our behaviour in the present. Exercise 17.5 is an individual and group exercise looking at ways in which participants can support themselves.

Exercise 17.3 *Time: 45 min.*

THOUGHT PATTERNS

Description An individual written exercise exploring patterns of thought at moments of particular stress or difficulty.

Aims To identify recurring patterns of thought. To explore how these influence behaviour. To explore possible interventions in patterns that need to be changed.

Directions

1 You will need a flipchart and marker pen, plus A4 paper and pens for the group. Introduce the exercise by explaining the ideas outlined in the notes.   *5 min.*

2 Ask each participant to think of a recent situation in which they felt angry or resentful and their reactions were not totally under control. The best situations to work with are those which were left unresolved, and in which the participant feels that their responses followed a familiar, habitual pattern. Ask participants to divide a sheet of paper into three columns, headed (from left to right) FEELINGS, THOUGHTS and ANALYSIS. The middle column should be widest. In this column they will write down every thought they had during the incident and number the thoughts as they occurred. (See the example on page 137.) Their aim here is simply to produce a record of their *thoughts*, without explanations, justifications or moral judgments. They should not record actions or emotions at this stage. Ask participants to write down the thoughts that they can readily recall – this is not a memory-testing exercise.   *10 min.*

3 Ask participants to record their *feelings* at each stage in the left-hand column. (See the example.)   *5 min.*

4 In the right-hand column, participants record their analysis of what they were *doing* with their thoughts, concentrating on: thoughts which justified feelings or actions; thoughts which provoked escalation of the situation; and personal interventions made to halt the progression of thoughts. (See the example.)   *5 min.*

5 Ask one participant to volunteer their thought pattern for the group to look at, and write it up. Go through it with the group, looking at how the thoughts and feelings relate to each other, where the feelings and justifications coincide, and what kind of interventions happened or could have happened. How did they try to stop the build-up of angry or resentful thoughts? How else could they have helped themselves?   *10 min.*

6   Ask participants to look at their thought pattern and underline any points where they feel it would have been possible for them to react in a different way. What thoughts would have helped them to react differently?   *5 min.*

Feedback and discussion   What did participants learn about themselves? How could this kind of exercise help them to deal with tough situations?   *5 min.*

Notes   This exercise explores the thought patterns that lead people to behave in ways they are not happy with and which they feel they are not entirely in control of. It serves as an introduction to the exploration of the patterns of thinking and feeling that prevent us from changing the things we want

to change. Such patterns often control our lives, but it is possible to intervene in our own psychological habits and regain control. This exercise is a tester of how this can happen. It is one which needs to be used daily if we want to break the thought habits of a lifetime. With a group that will be together for some time, the exercise could be regularly repeated. Individuals might find it useful to keep a daily journal of their thought patterns in 'high-risk' situations – that is, for instance, ones in which they feel angry, frustrated, withdrawn or aggressive.

The exercise can make a valuable contribution to work with young people. It explores how they can change their lives, and empowers them to take control.

This exercise relates directly to the next one, THE SURVIVAL GAME. The two work well when explored together.

Skills   Analysis. Awareness.

Example 17.3

THOUGHT PATTERNS

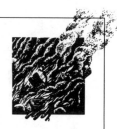

Situation Argument with a grumpy ticket collector on the underground who assumed that, because I was buying an excess fare ticket, I had tried to dodge the fare.

Feelings	Thoughts	Analysis
	1 This man is bloody grumpy.	
ANNOYED	2 He could at least be civil to me.	
INDIGNANT	3 It's not my fault there was no-one to buy a ticket from.	ENCOURAGING FEELING OF INDIGNATION
ANGRY	4 How dare he be so angry with me!	
	5 He's a grumpy old sod.	
SYMPATHETIC, PATRONISING	6 He's probably had a really bad day. He doesn't mean to be abusive.	ATTEMPTED INTERVENTION
INDIGNANT	7 I don't care if he's had a terrible day. He's rude and he's jumping to conclusions and he has no right to take his anger out on me.	
IN CONTROL	8 Calm down, Sue. He's had a bad day and you're tired too.	INTERVENTION
	9 Tell him you're sorry he's had a bad day.	
REJECTED	10 Well he's bloody ungrateful and stupid to shout at me when I'm trying to be helpful.	JUSTIFICATIONS FOR SHOUTING AT HIM
AFFRONTED, ANGRY	11 Stupid idiot. He doesn't deserve any sympathy. He's an arsehole.	
SELF-RIGHTEOUS	12 I want him to know I think he's an arsehole, 'cause he's a fucking grumpy mean old man and he's making me angry.	PASSING BLAME TO HIM – JUSTIFYING MY ANGER
ANGRY	13 I don't care how miserable he is. If I want to shout at him I will. He's made me angry.	
	14 Sod him – he deserves it.	FURTHER JUSTIFICATION FOR SHOUTING
UNEASY, ANNOYED WITH MYSELF	15 I'm glad I shouted at him.	
	16 He's an idiot – he deserved it.	

Exercise 17.4   *Time: 45 min.*

THE SURVIVAL GAME

Description   An individual and interactive exercise exploring how our interpretations of past events influence our behaviour in the present.

Aims   To distinguish between the facts of an event and the interpretation made of it. To identify some of the reasons why people make different interpretations of the same event. To explore the empowering effect of revising our personal interpretations of past events.

Directions

1   Introduce the participants to the ideas behind the exercise (see the notes).   *5 min.*

2   Ask each participant to think of an occasion on which their interpretation of an event coloured things thereafter. (For example, a colleague criticises something I have done with some young people, and I interpret this as meaning that he thinks I am an irresponsible worker. Everything he says to me now I interpret along those lines. Even when he praises me, I presume that it is because he is so surprised that I have done something worthy of praise.)   *5 min.*

3   Divide the group into pairs. Each person tells their partner about the event, and what they made it mean. They explore alternative interpretations, and consider what effect they could have had – and still could have.   *5 min.*

4   Divide the participants into small groups. Ask each group to create a tableau which is open to different interpretations. For example, someone holds their hand in the air looking at the person they are standing opposite. They may be about to hit the other person; they may be coming to greet them with a slap on the hand. (Maybe there are other interpretations too?)   *10 min.*

5   Each group shows their tableau to the other participants, who offer their interpretations.   *5 min.*

6   In the same small groups, participants address the following questions. (1) When working with young people, is there any kind of situation that you habitually interpret in a certain way? (2) What 'conversation' does this situation set off

in your head? (3) What 'conversation' could you have instead which would open up other possibilities for the situation? (For example, whenever a student asks me to explain something again, I have a conversation in my head which tells me that they couldn't be bothered to listen the first time. An alternative conversation might be one which tells me that they are keen and conscientious and want to learn. Changing that conversation in my head will totally change the way I respond to the situation in question. The aim is to create a 'new listening', and with it an inner voice which offers possibility rather than limitation.)   *10 min.*

7   If time allows, participants come together to hear an example of interpretive 'conversation', and possible ways of changing it, from each small group.

Feedback and discussion   How can participants use what they have learnt about themselves? How can it help them in dealing with tough situations? How can they develop the work for themselves outside the session or workshop?   *5 min.*

Notes   This exercise is based on ideas about the way we interpret what happens to us and what we see around us. The first premiss is that each of us is a survival machine, and that the instinct to survive affects our emotional as well as our physical well-being. The second premiss is that, when we feel hurt, disrespected or unloved the survival instinct leaps to our defence and helps us interpret whatever happened in a way which will protect us from further hurt (see Exercise 10.4). For example, a friend cancels a long-awaited meeting at the last minute. I interpret this as meaning that she is bored with our friendship and wants to end it. From now on I interpret everything she says as confirmation of my original interpretation.

When these things happen we have a conversation going on in our heads, pushing us in a particular direction. The conversation will sometimes help us to justify our interpretations and sometimes question them. These conversations are inspired by our outlook on life, so someone with low self-confidence may have a recurring conversation around themes such as 'They don't really think I'm any good' and 'I won't be so stupid as to be taken in by them', even when they are being praised or valued. This kind of conversation will protect someone against further hurt, but it will also prevent them seeing things from a different perspective – it might prevent them seeing the truth.

We all have our own ways of interpreting what happens to us, just as we all have habitual thought patterns (see Exercise 17.3). These habits of interpretation can be formed by accumulated incidents, or by one vital event. For example, a child who is never given any encouragement by their parents will at some point make a decision about what that means – perhaps 'They don't care, no-one cares.' The interpretation might bring with it a defensive resolve: 'I'm going to make sure I won't get hurt again.' So the child's interpretation of their parents' behaviour becomes a pair of glasses through which they view everything that happens to them. Any support or encouragement offered will have to get through the conversation in the head which is saying 'They don't mean it. They're only trying to break you down. Don't let them get to you.'

These two exercises (17.3 and 17.4) relate closely to one another. People who have thought patterns which lead consistently to violent or abusive behaviour are probably looking at the world through a pair of heavily tinted glasses, and listening to a loud conversation in the head which backs up their vision of things. But we all view the world through our own interpretive glasses.

This work is well worth doing with young people, but needs a safe environment with secure boundaries. Questioning our interpretations of the world, and of our own lives, is an immense challenge and should not be undertaken without suitable supportive structures.

It is important to make a distinction between what we do and do not have power over. We may not be able to change where we were born, or who our family is, or what has happened to us – our circumstances – but we *can* change what they mean to us and, therefore, how they will influence our future.

Skills Awareness. Analysis. Physical expression.

SUPPORT YOURSELF

Description An individual and group exercise looking at ways in which participants can support themselves and the tools they will need for doing it.

Aims To anticipate difficulties that participants are likely to face when they attempt to apply what they have learned from this course. To establish areas over which participants can take control, and to develop a structure for supporting their aims.

Directions

1 Brainstorm all the areas of difficulty that participants are likely to face when they try to incorporate the ideas that they have been exploring into their work. Include difficulties from outside (such as structures within the workplace) and difficulties that participants might face personally (controlling their own anger, perhaps, or becoming more assertive with a particular person).   *5 min.*

2 Brainstorm the word 'support'. What does support mean to the participants? How can they support themselves so that they don't give up when faced with difficulties?   *5 min.*

3 Divide participants into small groups to address the question of how each person can help themselves to stick to an ideal or commitment at difficult times – that is, how they can support themselves. Refer them to recent experiences such as failure to meet a deadline or difficulty in keeping a commitment to saving money. (At the end of the exercise is a suggested personal support structure for keeping on course when we feel we have failed in some way or mistakes have been made. It is discussed further in the notes.)   *20 min.*

Feedback and discussion Ask participants these questions. What do you usually do when you feel you have failed or made a mistake? What is the effect of taking responsibility rather than making excuses? What is difficult about it? In what ways does taking responsibility for mistakes and 'failures' give you support? How will you know that your personal support structures are intact and working? What will you do to mend them when they are not? What value do they have? What is the difference between taking responsibility and shouldering the blame?   *10 min.*

Session 18

Notes Taking responsibility for mistakes and failures is a way of reclaiming personal power, instead of handing it over to excuses and explanations. We keep it within our power to change things, or to make sure that the mistake is not made again. Taking responsibility is a very different act from 'shouldering the blame', which holds the person in the role of a victim. It is an act of self-empowerment. We may not have had control over what happened, but we can take control over how it affects us and how we deal with it.

Breakdowns happen only because a commitment has been made. Mistakes happen only when something has been tried that has not worked. Making commitments and taking responsibility for them can be empowering for the individual. Apportioning blame, finding fault, or making excuses has the opposite effect. Do we really want to give our circumstances such power over our lives?

Skills Imagination. Analysis. Creative thinking.

SUPPORT STRUCTURE

- Acknowledge what you have done.
- Accept responsibility for it.
- Clean up what you have done (that is, have any necessary conversations, clean up the mess).
- See what you can do to make sure it will not happen again.

Introduction Exploring various methods of reparation and recovery. Developing staff strategies for recovery from crisis situations. Developing negotiation skills.   *10 min.*

18.6	THE HANDSHAKE	*15 min.*
18.7	REPARATION, RECOVERY AND GAIN	*55 min.*
18.8	NEGOTIATING A WIN–WIN	*60 min.*

Reflection   *10 min.*

Notes Exercise 18.6 is an introductory group exercise looking at different ways of resolving disputes and hostilities. Exercise 18.7 is a group exercise to explore the concepts of recovery and reparation and to develop some practical strategies for the workplace. Exercise 18.8 is a small-group exercise putting into practice basic negotiating techniques, focusing on the preparation process.

THE HANDSHAKE

Description   An introductory group exercise looking at different methods to resolve disputes and hostilities.

Aims   To clarify the different methods of reconciliation. To explore what approaches are available to us.

Directions

Ask the group what methods can be used to bring two sides together, or to heal a rift between them. Write their responses up on a flipchart. Check what the group means by the terms used, and explain them to anybody who is not clear. Add any methods that have not been mentioned. (See the checklist on this page.) Good questions to ask: In what circumstances would you use each of these methods? What are the differences between them?   *10 min.*

Feedback and discussion   What negative or positive feelings do participants have about these methods? Why do they have those feelings? Have they experienced any of these methods? Can they see any practical use for any of them in their own environment?   *5 min.*

Notes   This is a very brief introduction to a complex area of work. The earlier in any dispute or conflict the proper techniques are used, the better it is for all concerned. Used early in the process, they can be peacekeeping agents in themselves. Used late in the day, they become healing agents. It would be very beneficial if people went to a mediator, counsellor or therapist in the same way that we attend the doctor or dentist. With conflict, as in healthcare, prevention is better than cure.

Skills   Discussion. Sharing. Debate.

CHECKLIST: RECONCILIATION METHODS

Mediation   Two parties come together willingly to settle their differences. One party will have approached a mediator. The agreements reached are created by the disputants themselves. The mediator merely facilitates the process, without giving advice or opinions. The agreements are not legally binding, but outline a way forward for the disputants.

Negotiation   Two parties negotiate directly over a decision or agreement that has to be made, or make use of a middle party who conducts the proceedings. Negotiations normally end with a binding contract.

Arbitration   Two parties agree on the appointment of an arbitrator, whose decision after consulting the disputing parties is binding.

Conciliation   A form of negotiation for resolving intense disputes.

Counselling   One-to-one sessions in which the counsellor helps the client to identify areas of concern and gain clarity and focus.

Therapy   One-to-one or in small groups. The therapist will challenge and probe to get an in-depth understanding of the difficulty or problem being investigated.

Reparation   Meetings between victim and attacker, held under the supervision of a counsellor or therapist. The aim is for both parties to find a way of dealing with their experience, and to attempt to heal the rift between them. The counsellor or therapist might see each party separately, for several sessions, before they are brought together.

Exercise 18.7 *Time: 55 min.*

REPARATION, RECOVERY AND GAIN

Description An exercise to explore the concepts of recovery and reparation and to develop some practical strategies for the workplace.

Aims To explore methods for staff recovery and reparation after a traumatic event in the workplace. To gain an understanding of the effects of traumatic events on the individual as well as within a staff group. To share how recovery and reparation methods could be used with young people themselves. To decide on practical ways of applying these methods.

Directions

1 Brainstorm the words 'reparation' and 'recovery' with the whole group. Write up all comments.   *5 min.*

2 In small groups, invite participants to talk about any traumatic event they have experienced in the workplace. Ask them to focus on the effects it had on them afterwards: the personal effects; the effects on their work; the effects on their relationships with colleagues, management, and young people; and the effect it had on their lives outside work.
                                                             15 min.

3 In the large group, ask small groups to feed back all the ideas they shared, ideally summarised into single words or short phrases.   *5 min.*

4 Again in small groups, ask members to focus on the methods of recovery that they used or might have used. Have any of them managed to heal the rift with the other party? If so, how? If methods were tried and failed, why did they not work?   *10 min.*

5 In the large group, get the small groups to report back on recovery and reparation strategies. The whole group could then look at practical methods by which staff members could receive support and other assistance, such as time off, counselling, compensation. What help is needed from outside? What help can be given by colleagues? What strategies could be implemented with young people, and practised to their benefit? Practical guidelines could now be drawn up, with specific reference to the workplace.   *15 min.*

Feedback and discussion What do participants feel they have gained from this exploration? What practical strategies have they formulated? What pleases them about the agreed plan of action? What further exploration would make them feel more secure and positive about their working environment?   *5 min.*

Notes In this exercise we are putting the subject of recovery and reparation on the agenda. It is important to emphasise the possibility of positive gain through this process. New strengths and new confidence can be built. Difficult and traumatic experiences can be put to constructive use. Like unresolved conflict, every crisis has a cost. Working on reparation and recovery is a way of finding the gains.

Skills Communication. Sharing. Analysis. Planning.

NEGOTIATING A WIN–WIN

Description   A small-group exercise in which participants practise basic negotiating techniques, with the focus on preparation.

Aims   To practise preparing for negotiation.

Directions

1   Participants work in pairs. One partner thinks of a situation that they would like to change through negotiation. Through their partner, they thoroughly prepare themselves for such a process. Give them this structure to follow:

a   Establish what your needs and fears are.

b   Establish what you think are the needs and fears of the other party. This can be done by talking through all the possibilities with your partner.

c   Establish what you want from the situation.

d   Decide the best way of getting it.

They now practise the negotiating process with their partner, stating their position clearly to the other party.   *10 min.*

2   The partners swap around, and repeat stage 1.   *10 min.*

3   It would now be a good idea for those who have completed this preparation to share with the rest of the group. Their feedback should be extremely brief, clear and precise – that is, needs and fears, what they want, how they will get it.   *10 min.*

4   Hand out copies of the NEGOTIATION GUIDELINES (page 144). Ask partners to work through this together, practising their own negotiation tactics in the light of it. How would they adapt these guidelines to their own situations? What are their ideal solutions? What would be realistic in the circumstances? What is their bottom line?   *20 min.*

Feedback and discussion   Do participants now feel prepared for real negotiation? In the simulation, what was the value of such thorough planning?   *10 min.*

Notes   It could be a good idea to have two participants role-play a negotiation, with a group of observers to give them feedback. (Extra time would have to be allocated.)

A natural extension of this exercise is to plan a large-group negotiation. Participants could role-play a management team and an employee team negotiating over working hours and conditions, with some members observing the proceedings. The two teams would then prepare separately, and could break to reassess and plan between each phase. The teams would have to give their members clear roles to ensure effective interaction during the process. Before the role-play begins, establish all the relevant details concerning the dispute and the personnel involved.

Skills   Planning. Anticipation. Tactical preparation. Understanding structure.

NEGOTIATION GUIDELINES

- Negotiation is more than reconciliation.

- Negotiation is about achieving an aim.

- Negotiation is often between two parties who might have different objectives but are willing to agree to a compromise.

- Negotiation can occur directly between the two parties in dispute, but can also take place through a negotiator who acts as a go-between.

- All negotiations have a common structure.

- The art of negotiating could be described as 'bargaining to achieve agreement'.

- Both parties must make realistic offers to get the process in motion. If there is no movement on either side, then both sides lose.

- If only one party is prepared to move, then you could have a situation where there is a winner and a loser.

- If you move too much without reciprocation, you have nothing left to bargain with.

- If both sides are prepared to move, then you have the possible basis for an agreement – a compromise. This could result in both parties winning.

- An offer could be phrased thus: 'If you give me some of what I want, then I'll give you some of what you want.'

- There are several stages in a negotiating process:
  1. Preparation – clarifying what you want and how you intend to get it.
  2. Discussions – each side states their position.
  3. Proposals tabled: 'What if . . . then perhaps'. Movement starts.
  4. Bargaining begins – give and take, moving towards each other.
  5. Coming to an agreement.

- It is important to establish what your targets are. What is the maximum to go for? What is the minimum to accept?

- Test the ground with tentative proposals. See what the response is.

- Give up what is easy for you in return for what is of value to you.

- Never concede anything without getting something in return.

- Value every offer you make in the other party's terms. What does it mean to them? Think yourself into their position. The better you understand their position, the better equipped you are for the negotiating process. This is sometimes called 'second guessing'.

- What is your ideal solution?

- What would be a realistic solution?

- What is your fall-back position, your bottom line?

- Do not assume that the first thing asked for by the other party is necessarily the most important thing in their terms.

- The final stage of a negotiation is very important. Put the agreement in writing. There can easily be different interpretations of what has been written, so the wording of the agreement is critical.

- A good way of evaluating your own preparation is to check whether your second guessing was equal to the ideal solution of the other party.

MEDIATION

The ritual of reconciliation

MEDIATION
The ritual of reconciliation

You can't shake hands with a clenched fist.

Indira Gandhi

THE aim of the mediation process is to encourage disputants to 'unclench their fists' and to reach out to one another. Mediation is a way of helping those who are in conflict to resolve their differences by talking to each other. It involves mediators, people who are trained to listen to those in conflict and to help them resolve their disagreements. They facilitate reconciliation by creating space and a supportive framework within which those in disagreement can resolve the problem themselves, and so take ownership of their solution. A mediator is not there to give advice.

Those in conflict are referred to as the disputants, or the parties. Mediators do not take sides or force the parties into anything. Their ultimate goal is to help the disputants find their own solution to the situation, one which they are prepared to uphold in the future. This is termed an agreement. Mediation is never imposed on the disputants – they make use of it only if they wish to do so.

With young people, mediation can be used in peer disputes, group disputes, and between young people and adults, perhaps staff and students. A challenging facet of mediation training is that it can be directed towards young people themselves, helping them to acquire the skills to mediate in peer disputes. (In disputes between adults and young people it is better to have a team of mediators working together, a young person and an adult, thus providing a positive and balanced role model.) Very few young people will go on to become professional mediators, but the skills acquired through this training can be invaluable in everyday living. Young people who learn that there are two sides to every dispute, and many different approaches to resolving them, have learnt a tremendous amount.

These are some of the key assumptions made in mediation training with young people:

- that conflict is an unavoidable part of living which can be used as an opportunity for learning and personal growth
- that, since conflict is unavoidable, learning conflict resolution skills is as 'educational' and as essential to young people as the learning of history or mathematics
- that young people can resolve their conflicts as effectively with the assistance of other young people as they can with the assistance of adults – and sometimes more effectively
- that encouraging young disputants to collaborate in the resolution of present conflict is an effective method of preventing future conflict and developing responsibility

MEDIATION
The ritual of reconciliation

An American trainer, Richard Cohen, comments: 'There is something very liberating about young people and adults learning together. An atmosphere is created in which boundaries are relaxed and each group gains a new appreciation of the abilities and the integrity of the other.'

In this section we are devoting only seven and a half hours to mediation. It is merely an introduction to the techniques and the discipline involved. Thorough mediation training could easily involve another 60-hour course. Many of the skills needed for mediation are covered in the wide range of exercises and experiences offered by this training course, but there are certain specific mediation skills and techniques that are beyond its scope.

This section contains three two-and-a-half-hour sessions. Session 19 is an introduction to mediation – its function and the skills needed. Session 20 looks at the mediation process, and includes the preparation of a mediation role-play. Session 21 focuses on mediation in practice, involving practical experience through role-play.

All training techniques (such as brainstorm, role-play and tableau work) are explained in TRAINING FOR TRAINERS.

Session 19

Introduction
Uses and functions of mediation, and the skills needed. Active listening, extracting important points, creative use of information received. *20 min.*

19.1	ACTIVE LISTENING IN MEDIATION	*30 min.*
19.2	CAUGHT IN THE MIDDLE	*35 min.*
19.3	GETTING TO YES	*40 min.*
19.4	THE RITUAL OF MEDIATION	*15 min.*

Reflection *10 min.*

Notes Exercise 19.1 is a warm-up exercise focusing on active listening and feedback. Exercise 19.2 creates a pressurised situation in which two mediators have to steer the dispute towards a satisfactory conclusion. Exercise 19.3 creates another pressurised situation during which the mediators contribute to the resolution of a dispute by giving 'clients' the support they need in order to resolve the dispute positively for themselves. Exercises 19.2 and 19.3 involve role-play. Exercise 19.4 is an introduction to the specific stages of the mediation process, in preparation for the next two sessions.

Exercise 19.1 *Time: 30 min.*

ACTIVE LISTENING IN MEDIATION

Description A listening exercise in pairs for use in mediation training.

Aims To practise gathering information – teasing out the issues and the subtext of the dispute.

Directions

1 Ask each participant to think of a conflict situation that they are currently involved in, one in which they feel their point of view has not been understood. It could be a situation in which they are facing anger, or some incident that they are not feeling happy about. Divide the group into pairs. *5 min.*

2 In each pair, partner A describes their incident to B. Partner B listens without comment, though nods and other gestures of encouragement might reassure A that they have B's attention. *5 min.*

3 B briefly feeds back the information learned from A, to let A know that they have gathered the basics of the situation. Then B draws out of A what their feelings and needs are in the situation. At this point B is making careful guesses based on what has already been learned from A (see the notes). Allow time for feedback within the pairs, focusing on whether A felt that B's observations were accurate. *5 min.*

4 Ask As and Bs to swap roles and repeat the above procedure. *10 min.*

Feedback and discussion Did participants find their partners successful in understanding their feelings and needs? What difficulties did they experience in getting to the roots of their own partners' needs and feelings? What was the effect of having the subtext of their words understood? *5 min.*

Notes The aim in active listening is to tease out the subtext of the conflict, asking questions if you need to clarify the situation. Look for the speaker's priorities. What is the real issue for them? Focus on what the speaker feels rather than what they think.

Skills Concentrated listening. Listening without judgment. Drawing out information. Summing up. Giving feedback.

Caught in the Middle

Description   A small-group exercise looking at negotiation and mediation skills.

Aims   To develop and practise mediation and negotiation skills under pressure.

Directions

1   Divide participants into teams of four. From each team, two protagonists stand at either side of the room facing each other. Each protagonist has a messenger or negotiator standing between themselves and the other protagonist. Give each protagonist a card representing both sides of the dispute in which they are involved. (For example: (A) You want to use the car for leisure activity two nights a week. You feel you deserve the use of the car after a hard day's work. (B) You want the car on the same two nights each week to attend evening classes. It is difficult to get home from the college, and you feel your classes are more important than your partner's leisure activities.)   *5 min.*

2   The protagonists decide who will start. There is no planning or liaison with the messengers. Protagonist A tells their messenger what they would like to say to Protagonist B. Messenger A then passes this information on to Messenger B, who in turn passes it on to Protagonist B. Protagonist B tells their response to their messenger, who follows the process in reverse.   *10 min.*

3   As the dispute hots up, ask the messengers to start to take on mediator roles. They now start to consult with each other and decide what suggestions they should put to their respective clients. They do not consult with their clients, but work out a tactic, try it out, get a response, and then report back to the other messenger. Working together in this way, they help their clients to come to some agreement which benefits both parties.

   The negotiators should keep their consultations in the middle brief. A timekeeper could help keep up the pressure and pace of the negotiation.

4   Participants swap roles and repeat the exercise, using new cards.   *10 min.*

Feedback and discussion   How well did the negotiators work as a team? Did they manage to bring the disputants to a resolution? What techniques did they use in trying to resolve the dispute? What worked well? What approaches didn't work? How did the negotiators experience the pressure of time?

10 min.

Notes   This exercise focuses on building teamwork and strategies for advancing a dispute towards a resolution. The experience of working under pressure in pairs is a useful preparation for running a formal mediation session. Feedback from observers can be useful.

Skills   Teamwork. Role-play and improvisation. Problem-solving. Listening and observation. Developing tactics. Clarity and brevity.

Exercise 19.3 *Time: 40 min.*

GETTING TO YES

Description   A small-group exercise looking at mediation and negotiation skills.

Aims   To develop and practise mediation and negotiation skills in an active way and under the pressure of time. To learn to take advice selectively, and to put advice into action.

Directions

1   Put participants into groups of four, and divide each group into two pairs. Have one protagonist and a helper in each pair. Give each pair a card representing the two sides of the dispute. (For example: (A) Your next-door neighbour gets in late and plays music till the early hours. You get up early in the morning and can't sleep. (B) Your neighbour gets up early every morning and takes the dog for a walk. The dog barks excitedly every morning and wakes you up. You work a late shift and get in at midnight. It takes you a couple of hours to unwind, have a snack and get to sleep. *Context:* Tension has been on the increase in recent weeks and the atmosphere is acrimonious.) Independently, the two pairs prepare for the role-play. How can they get their neighbour to stop what is clearly an unsociable activity?   *10 min.*

2   Call the first round. The two protagonists enter the 'ring' and the dispute begins. The helpers remain outside the ring in their respective 'corners' and closely observe the performance of their partners. Call the end of the round when you think a good exchange has taken place.   *10 min.*

3   In the break, the helper has a few moments to give their partner feedback and some quick advice as to the way forward in the next round. The protagonist just listens.

4   Call the next round and let the dispute continue. The disputants try to follow the advice of their corners as well as trying to respond to all the tactics of their opponent.

5   Call the next break, and the helpers resume their corner duties. This process can continue until an end result is achieved. The result might be a good working agreement, a stalemate, or a victory for one of the protagonists (that is, getting the other side to agree while conceding nothing themselves). You, as timekeeper, decide when the bout ends.

6   Try a second dispute, swapping roles. In each dispute allow about six minutes for role-play and four minutes for feedback in small groups.   *10 min.*

Feedback and discussion   How well did the disputants absorb and use their instructions? How appropriate was the advice given? What were the difficulties of giving and absorbing advice under pressure?   *10 min.*

Notes   The exercise can be run with one or two observers in each corner. Their role would be to observe how well the disputants absorb and use the corner instructions. The disputants could ask the observers how appropriate their corner's advice was, and how clearly it was given. The observers could thus lead the feedback. If there were no observers, the timekeeper could lead the discussion. The whole group could focus on all the tactics that were used – which were appropriate, and what types and styles of approach were effective. By getting feedback from observers, helpers and protagonists, the group should be able to develop a good overall picture of the dispute.

The use of a metaphorical wrestling or boxing ring provides a clearly defined space in which the dispute can take place. It also provides a clear structure – the use of a 'referee', of 'corners', of 'coaches', of rules and timekeeping. And it provides a sense of urgency and action. There is a strict no-physical-contact rule in this exercise. The conflict resolution techniques being practised obviously bear no resemblance to the win-at-all-costs violence of a wrestling or boxing bout.

Skills   Role-play and improvisation. Listening and observation. Decision-making. Developing tactics. Taking instructions and using advice.

Exercise 19.4   *Time: 15 min.*

THE RITUAL OF MEDIATION

Description   Group exploration of the core concepts of mediation.

Aims   To cover the basic steps of the mediation process. To highlight the core concepts underpinning the process of mediation.

Directions

1   Explain to the group the basic steps in the mediation process:

- *Opening statement*   Introductions, welcomes, confidentiality, ground rules.
- *Listening to what happened*   Each party speaks; summarise what you heard.
- *Stating what each person wants*   Ask questions to clarify, then summarise, each party's goals.
- *Finding solutions*   Establishing what each person is prepared to do; finding solutions that are specific, balanced and real.
- *Coming to agreement*   Review points of agreement; agreement is confirmed.
- *Closing statement*   Affirmation, conclusion, thanks.
- *Follow through*   Monitoring of the agreement; evaluation of the process.   *5 min.*

2   Cover the basic concepts underlying the process:

- Confidentiality.
- Ground rules – abuse, interruptions, physical violence, etc.
- Voluntary process.
- Agreements are not legally binding.
- Agreements are the result of the disputants' work.
- Mediators are not there to give advice or act as judges of what is right and wrong. A mediator is not an expert or an authority figure.
- Mediators are people who have been trained to help people find ways to resolve their conflicts. They encourage people to work through their problems and reach agreements that are workable for them.
- Mediators do not take sides in disputes, but strive to remain impartial at all times. They should keep their own opinions and beliefs to themselves.   *5 min.*

Feedback and discussion   Allow a little time for questions about the mediation process – its function, its benefits, its uses, its difficulties – and give examples of successful mediation processes.   *5 min.*

Notes   The purpose of this session is to create an interest in the subject of mediation. Try asking group members to talk about occasions where they felt they acted as mediators, whether formally or informally. Unlike other exercises, this one is in the style of a brief introduction and presentation. It provides the basis for the next session, which looks at all the stages in detail.

Session 20

Introduction The stages of the mediation process, and how they work. Preparing a dispute for mediation. *10 min.*

20.5 Introducing the stages of mediation *65 min.*
20.6 Role-play for mediation *65 min.*

Reflection *10 min.*

Notes In Exercise 20.5 participants look in detail at how the various stages in the mediation process work. This is groundwork for Exercise 20.6, in which participants prepare a dispute that will be mediated in the next session.

Exercise 20.5 *Time: 65 min.*

INTRODUCING THE STAGES OF MEDIATION

Description A large-group exploration of the content of each stage of the mediation process.

Aims To acquaint the group with the content of each stage of the mediation process. To develop a checklist for the group to use at each stage. To give examples to the group of the details of specific stages.

Directions

1 Take the participants through Handout 20.5A, TRAINING GUIDELINES FOR MEDIATION (pages 154–155). *20 min.*

2 Share with participants the example of a detailed summary given on Handout 20.5B, LESLEY GERRA'S FIRST STATEMENT (page 156). Here the mediator summarises the facts after careful listening, giving one disputant the feeling that they have been listened to, and the other disputant another chance to listen to the other point of view.

Also hand out and share the example of an agreement (Handout 20.5C, page 157). *10 min.*

3 Encourage the participants, in small groups or in pairs, to examine the guidelines again and develop a checklist that they could use in the next session to practise a mediation. (If they work in pairs, it is a good idea for them to stay in the same pairs for the subsequent role-play and mediation exercise. In this way they can establish good working relationships.)
  15 min.

4 All come together and get a couple of participants to share their checklists. Others can comment – perhaps to point out any missing items. *10 min.*

Feedback and discussion Check that all participants are clear about each of the stages and its content. Check that they are all confident with their checklists. *10 min.*

Notes A good way to demonstrate the stages of the mediation process would be for the two facilitators to perform a role-play. By freezing the action and using commentary or narration, it is possible to 'cut' from one important moment to another, showing the shifts and development in the process.

TRAINING GUIDELINES FOR MEDIATION

I   THE COMPLAINT

1   Contact with the first party, by letter, phone, visit to mediation service. Hear problem.

2   Explain the process of mediation and the role of mediators. Note that mediation is a free service.

3   Stress voluntariness, confidentiality, freedom to withdraw or complain, and the primacy of listening, communication, and problem-solving.

4   Agreement that the second party (or parties) should be contacted – first by letter, then by phone (if possible).

II   THE SECOND PARTY

1   Visit by the service's co-ordinator, or an experienced volunteer, to the second party.

2   Building on what has been said by letter or phone, explain the role of mediation and the functions of the mediators, who they are and who they are not (police, for instance).

3   Hear something of the second party's involvement in the dispute.

4   Stressing the benefits of resolving the conflict, gain voluntary agreement to a mediation session.

III   FIRST MEDIATION SESSION

1   Introductions. Agreement on surnames or first names for the session.

2   Reminder of what has taken place so far, by way of contacts, and that both parties have met because they wish to resolve the problem or dispute.

3   Outline of ground rules. Secure agreement to each before proceeding: keep seated; do not interrupt; avoid insulting language; allow the mediators to intervene and prohibit anything that they consider

unacceptable; smoking allowed or not; all will respect confidentiality, mediators and disputants.

4   Explain the process:
- A chance for each disputant to describe, from the beginning, all that has happened to bring the parties into this situation.
- Mediator will clarify and agree with each party the correctness of each statement by reflecting it back.
- A chance, then, for the disputants to talk together and for the mediators to help in clarifying the issues and the feelings involved.
- The finding of some common ground upon which agreement can be reached, hopefully to be written up so that everyone can sign.
- Each disputant to have the opportunity at any time of going into caucus (private session) with the mediators.
- Agreements are not legally binding.

5   Hear the statements of each of the parties. Attempt to discover as many of the facts and issues as possible, and some of the feelings involved. Try to get some sense of what each party wants to get out of the session, and what they will settle for.

6   Reflect back the statements, each in turn. Objectively summarise all relevant facts, issues, feelings. Aim to lay all the ingredients of the dispute on the table, so that each party is fully informed of the other's complaints.

IV   INTERACTION BETWEEN THE CONTENDING PARTIES

1   Change the seating pattern so that the disputants face each other, rather than the mediators. Invite dialogue and questioning, but still within the ground rules.

2   Mediators keep good processes to the fore, 'actively' listening and reflecting back the subtext. They tease out the issues and encourage disputants to express their feelings.

3 Affirming the contributions and achievements of the disputants.

4 Consolidate any apology or concession and make sure that the other party has heard it.

5 Tackle the easiest issue first. Agreeing one point helps in gaining agreement on other points. If one party offers a concession, it helps the second party to offer one in turn.

6 If one party says something important to a mediator, ask them to say it directly to the other party.

V POSSIBLE CAUCUS – EACH PARTY HEARD SEPARATELY

1 If there is still blocking or lack of trust, it may be helpful at any time for the mediators to work with each party alone. The mediators may see that there is an underlying problem which is handicapping the communication, perhaps because it is too painful or confidential, and which needs to be aired in confidence.

2 As in stage III, each party is heard in depth and actively listened to, but is encouraged to explore feelings.

VI NEGOTIATION AND DISCOVERING COMMON GROUND – POSSIBLE SECOND SESSION

1 The two parties and the mediators might be reconvened on a second occasion. Any fresh information or points of view are now shared between the parties, with the aim of bringing about some deeper understanding of the issues.

2 Reflection by each party on what they have heard. Attempt to get each party to feel what it is like to be in the other's shoes.

3 General movement from the conflict to the problems behind it and the discovering of any common ground.

4 One of the parties may say that something was done in the heat of the moment. This could be developed into an apology or an approximation to one.

5 Attempts at problem-solving. What can we do about the situation? How to defuse it? Possible brainstorm. Creative solutions. Give-and-take. Emotion has now been taken out of the issue and the focus is on resolution and reparation.

6 Start moving towards an agreement, if this now seems appropriate. First list those items that oblige *both* parties to do something.

7 Next list individual obligations agreed to, alternating them A then B. Start with the least onerous agreements first. Try to include undertakings by both parties in the agreement. Parties must feel that they have gained something specific, such as a concession, from the mediation. (They may also need to sell the agreement as a success to other people – the other members of their household, for instance.)

VII SIGNING THE CONTRACT AND FOLLOW-UP

1 Read out final contract to both parties. Make any amendments necessary for final agreement.

2 Both parties now sign three copies of the agreement, and each take a copy home. One copy remains with the mediators as a record. It should be stressed that this is not legally binding, but is signed in good faith.

3 Any ritual or symbol of conclusion – shaking hands, perhaps coffee together.

4 The mediators seek permission to contact both parties after an agreed period, a month or so, to see how the arrangements are working out.

5 Possible talk about how the mediation has gone, and reflection for the mediators. Everything but the contract will now be shredded for confidentiality.

LESLEY GERRA'S FIRST STATEMENT
As repeated by a mediator

YOU moved into Hamilton Lane full of enthusiasm. It was the first time you had set up home away from your parents' house in St Albans. You had taken out a high mortgage on a redeveloped property, buying it freehold, and you had just started in a good new post as assistant editor of a catering journal.

You first met your neighbour Colin McDermot on the day you moved in. He and some of his friends were outside his ground-floor flat, which is on the west side of your own. You said you were conscious of them making loud remarks about the furniture as it came out of the van, and they all laughed and cheered when something fell and was smashed. You said you felt scared by them and wondered what you had let yourself in for.

Within days, you said, you began to be disturbed in the early hours of the morning by arrivals next door, leading to loud laughter and at times to music from a ghetto-blaster. You said that some days later you began to be disturbed by the noise of Colin leaving the flat about dawn and the starting of a car.

You several times went to talk it through but could never find him in. Once, unable to stand it any more, you banged on the wall, but you said this only made matters worse as someone banged back more loudly and the music seemed to get louder.

You said other incidents occurred. Your milk bottles have been broken. Sometimes your milk wasn't there and you assumed it was stolen. Flowers were pulled up from the new window boxes you had installed and planted. You said litter and rubbish from the dustbins in Colin's entrance spilled into your own gateway. You said you object to the general dilapidation of the front of his house, and thought at first that it was a squat. You thought that Colin might be unemployed.

During the summer months, you said, there was trouble over the fence between the small gardens at the rear of both flats, which are used by the ground-floor occupants only. While entertaining friends you found Colin and his friends in their back garden, talking loudly, and making fun of your friends, their accents and what they were saying. This became progressively worse, your friends felt harassed, and you have had to stop arranging such occasions. However, you recently held a St Valentine's Day barbecue, and you said that the abuse became intolerable. When some of your friends started retaliating, they had rubbish thrown at them and a whole dustbin of rubbish was tipped over the fence. The barbecue had to be abandoned and you said you had every intention of going to the police but held back because you didn't want to make matters worse.

This last incident precipitated your visit to the mediation centre.

You said you now feel desperate. You wonder about moving away, but feel that would be to give in. You said you need to write at home sometimes, for your work and also because you want to begin on a book, but you find you cannot concentrate and get too angry.

You don't know what to do and feel you are living in fear of being physically molested. You feel you have done nothing to deserve this kind of treatment.

THE AGREEMENT

A G R E E M E N T

between
Lesley Gerra and Colin McDermot

We have taken part in a mediation session and we have voluntarily agreed to the following:

1 Colin agrees to ask his friends not to give Lesley any verbal abuse.

2 Lesley agrees to ensure that when her friends visit they will not park in front of Colin's flat.

3 Lesley and Colin both agree to make every attempt to prevent music being played at unsociable levels at unsociable hours.

4 Colin and Lesley both agree to organise parties so that they don't clash, and will warn each other when such plans are being started.

5 Lesley and Colin both agree to deal with any future annoyance when it occurs, and to come to an agreement by discussion rather than by argument.

6 Colin and Lesley both agree to give their individual support to the talked-about possible development of a residents' association for Hamilton Lane, in the hope of some improvements to the state of the road and some of its properties.

We believe that this agreement is fair, and we agree to live up to it.

Signed: _____   Signed: _____
Colin McDermot   Lesley Gerra

Date: _____   Date: _____

Exercise 20.6   *Time: 65 min.*

ROLE-PLAY FOR MEDIATION

Description   An exercise in pairs to develop and prepare a role-play.

Aims   To develop role-plays that can be used in the following session for mediation practice. To prepare in pairs the order and process of the mediation.

Directions

1   In pairs, partners prepare a dispute which will be mediated by another pair in the following session. They need to develop and establish: two characters in dispute; a situation of dispute; specific incidents to talk about; specific grievances against each other; what they want from the mediation process; and some sticking points – things that their characters might not wish to compromise about. If they wish, the partners could keep some of these details from each other and reveal them in the role-play.

The facilitator should check that all the pairs have made specific decisions and are clear about what they are doing.

35 min.

2   In the same pairs, participants prepare their strategy for the mediation that they will be facilitating in the next session. Things they need to determine or rehearse are: the order and content of the introduction; how they will present it; which partner will start and explain the first stage; which partner will give the first feedback; the process, all the way down to securing the agreement at the end of the mediation; how they will seat themselves; and any notetaking. Partners should practise presenting the introduction to each other. They should also practise giving instructions to each other.   *15 min.*

3   A few participants should practise giving the introduction and instructions to the whole group. Other participants might like to comment, perhaps suggesting improvements.   *10 min.*

Feedback and discussion   Make sure that all participants are clear about the role-play and the mediation that they will run in the next session.   *5 min.*

Notes   An alternative way of preparing for the role-play is to hand out sheets with characters and disputes clearly worked out. Then the participants will only need to be briefed and

helped to clarify their roles and the situation. This could be easier, and would suit less experienced groups.

It helps if the characters in the role-play are based on the participants themselves. The purpose of the role-play is to service the mediation and to provide good practice for the two trainee mediators, which calls for a good and consistent dispute. The focus is not on the performing abilities or the wit of the role-players.

Here are some useful questions to help create the role-plays:

* What was the incident that led you to mediation?
* What has your relationship with the other party been like in the past (both before and after the incident)?
* What initial position is your character going to take?
* What do you think your character really wants from mediation?
* What is your character feeling at the beginning of the session?
* How much are you going to say in the joint session? Are there things that you are going to keep secret until the caucus? Are there things that you are never going to tell?

Session 21

Introduction

Introduction Reminder of the important stages, of the ways of running the session and interacting with the disputants.

10 min.

21.7 MEDIATION IN PRACTICE   *130 min.*

Reflection   *10 min.*

Notes In teams of four (two disputants and two mediators), participants have a chance to practice mediation skills. The disputants will have prepared their role-played dispute in the previous session.

Exercise 21.7 *Time: 130 min.*

MEDIATION IN PRACTICE

Description A practical exercise in fours to practise mediation skills.

Aims To give all participants a chance to try mediation. To practise skills necessary for good mediation.

Directions

1 Divide participants into groups of four, each made up of two of the pairs established in the previous session. Let each group decide which pair will mediate first and which will role-play their dispute for mediation. Each pair should briefly prepare. The role-players should remind themselves of the details concerning their characters and the situation. They should use notes in the role-play as a reminder if necessary. The two mediators can quickly remind themselves of the order of doing things and what they will say in terms of introductions and key instructions.   *5 min.*

2 The role-play and mediation can begin. The facilitators should rove around monitoring the process, intervening only where appropriate (see *TRAINING FOR TRAINERS*, pages 19–20). If there are an odd number of participants, anyone not included should work as an observer. This can be an important task. Getting objective outside feedback can be very valuable for all the participants. Observers can also learn a great deal from others' good practice and mistakes.   *45 min.*

3 In fours, the groups can reflect on the mediation, giving each other comments and feedback. The facilitator should rove around to monitor and assist this process. Key questions could be: What worked for you as a mediator? What didn't work for you as a mediator? What would you like to improve next time and how? How did you work with your partner? What worked and didn't work for you as a disputant? What could you improve in your role-play? How? How did the role-players feel they sustained their roles? How did the mediators feel the role-play worked?   *10 min.*

4 In each group, the pairs now swap over and prepare for their new tasks, mediators becoming role-players, and role-players mediators. They should try to use whatever they have learnt from the brief feedback session.   *5 min.*

5 The second mediation.   *45 min.*

6 A short feedback in the groups of four, using the same
questions as before.   *10 min.*

Feedback and discussion The whole group can share
responses to the questions considered in the two small-group
feedbacks. It would also be interesting to hear from the
observers. The facilitators should then give their own feedback
to the whole group. It should be stressed to participants that
mediation is a well-defined and a demanding process, one that
it takes time and practice to become comfortable with. *10 min.*

Notes Listening as a mediator takes a great deal of energy
and concentration, and can be exhausting. When mediators
speak, they do so purposefully, and without cross-examining
or putting the disputants on the defensive. The whole
mediation process is one that needs considerable practice for
all parties to feel comfortable within the structure, and to be
able to use it to its full potential. The checklist might help.

CHECKLIST FOR MEDIATORS

*You **listen** in order to:*

- discover the underlying causes of the conflict
- discover the parties' interests
- discover what the parties have in common
- discover room for movement
- observe a softening of attitudes
- observe a readiness to settle

*You **speak** in order to:*

- set the parties at ease
- make sure the process is clear
- show that you are listening and that you understand what has been said
- help the parties hear one another

- manage tensions between the parties
- test the parties' receptiveness to various options
- help the parties see reality
- share positive accomplishments
- keep up the disputants' morale

The agreement

- Is the resolution specific enough? Does it say what/ when/where/who/how?
- Is the resolution balanced? Do both disputants share the responsibility for making it work?
- Can both disputants really do what they promise?
- Will the resolution solve the problem?
- Will the resolution solve the problem for good?

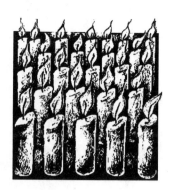

SOCIAL CHANGE

Towards community action

SOCIAL CHANGE
Towards community action

Just as we are all fuel for fires that can burn and destroy, so are we fuel for fires that can light our lives and warm our hearts. A spark lands on dry tinder and starts off the fire. It spreads and becomes a blaze. The blaze rejuvenates the ageing soil and offers us possibilities of new growth. It is a bright beacon. The flames dance with energy and opportunity.

THE fire analogy can represent co-operation and creation as well as conflict and destruction:

THE FUEL   The people, as before, who live and work with each other.

THE SPARK   A raw issue brings a flash of new insight to a community. It is taken up by the live-wire, who initiates a plan to bring about change.

SMOULDERING   The idea is mulled over and talked about. It is picked up by others, who persist in encouraging yet others to think about it, to respond.

FANNING THE FLAMES   Strength is gathered when new people join in, with skills in solving problems. They give life to the slow-burning fire.

STOKING THE FIRE   Consolidating what has been gained, the advocates and the trail-blazers pile on encouragement and support for action.

THE BLAZE   Finally the stoked fire bursts into great flames. The beacon has been lit. It is a light that will not go out. It gives warmth, energy and inspiration.

The creative blaze is the work of live-wires, initiators, persisters and peace-makers. They spark, smoulder, fan and stoke, as do the agitators and provokers of conflict. Their behaviour is regenerative. The blaze brings new challenge, with change and rejuvenation. We are all fuel; we are all potential beacon-builders.

Focus   Exploring intervention in situations of intense conflict. Exploring non-violent options. Exploring strategies for social change.

Aims   To explore the nature of intervention. To explore what it means to take sides and the difficulties of making a stand. To explore the possibilities of non-violence. To create a personal strategy for bringing about social change.

Key concepts   Non-violence. Intervention. Taking sides. Social change.

Key questions   What does it mean to take sides in a conflict? What are the non-violent options available to us? Do different crises require different intervention strategies? What can I do as one individual to bring about social change?

This section contains three two-and-a-half-hour sessions. Session 22 uses the fire analogy as a structure for intervention in conflicts. Session 23 explores situations of intense conflict and examines alternatives to violence as means of bringing about change. Session 24 looks at stages for bringing about social change.

All training techniques (such as brainstorm, role-play and tableau work) are explained in TRAINING FOR TRAINERS.

Session 22

Introduction
Positive intervention in situations of conflict.

10 min.

22.1 CONFLICT IN ACTION: INTERVENTION FOR CHANGE

130 min.

Reflection
10 min.

Notes Exercise 22.1 uses the fire analogy, exploring all the possible types of intervention and how different types will be appropriate at different stages of the conflict. It is a practical exercise using role-play.

Exercise 22.1 *Time: 130 min.*

CONFLICT IN ACTION: INTERVENTION FOR CHANGE

Description An exercise using role-play to enact the progression of a particular conflict, with the purpose of exploring how intervention could have affected the eventual destructive or negative outcome.

Aims To explore the fire analogy as a practical tool in conflict resolution. To look at all the different stages in a conflict where positive intervention is possible. To see how the nature of the intervention will differ depending on the stage of the conflict.

Directions

1 Making use of the handout entitled FIRE, CONFLICT AND CHANGE (see page 7), remind participants of the stages of the fire analogy. Ask every participant to think of a conflict that they have been involved in, or one that they are very familiar with. They should ideally choose one that developed over a period of time, with fairly clear points of progression, not a conflict that flared up immediately and was all over in a couple of minutes. Every member will try to subdivide their conflict under each of the headings of the fire analogy. They will need to skip a stage if it is not appropriate.   *15 min.*

2 This work can be shared by the large group or, if the group is too large, in smaller groups of four or five members. Each small group will then choose one of the conflicts to dramatise in order to share it with the larger group.   *15 min.*

3 During the preparation participants need to consider all the points at which intervention could be successful, and how different kinds of intervention will be appropriate at different stages. (A conflict which has reached the blazing stage, for instance, will require more radical forms of intervention than a smouldering situation.)   *30 min.*

4 The groups show their role-plays. (If there is only one large group, the facilitators function as the audience.) They then select one scene or section and ask the audience for suggestions as to how one character could intervene to make a positive contribution to the possible resolution of the conflict. The scene is replayed. The audience can call 'freeze' at any point and make a suggestion for one of the characters to try

---

CASE STUDIES USING THE FIRE ANALOGY

Immediate escalation of conflict

THE FUEL   Simon is a council worker and has been on strike for ten days. He is in a car with a colleague. They are on their way to a union meeting about the strike. It is a hot midsummer day and there is a lot of traffic on the road. They are in London.

THE SPARK   Simon's car runs out of petrol in a busy street.

SMOULDERING   There are shouts from the car behind because Simon is not moving on. Simon pushes his car to the side of the road.

FANNING THE FLAMES   The man in the car behind leans out and shouts abuse at Simon. Simon shouts abuse back.

STOKING THE FIRE   The man in the car behind gets out, comes over to Simon and spits at him.

THE BLAZE   Simon grabs a crowbar and badly beats up the man.

Notes   The man in the car was badly injured by Simon and there was evidence for a serious criminal charge against him. The police encouraged him to settle out of court and Simon wrote to the man explaining how he had been at the end of his tether. He apologised for what he had done and offered to pay damages for the man's clothes. The man replied, accepting Simon's apology, and the matter was ended. Simon felt that had he been taken to court there would have been no opportunity for him to explain and apologise, and he would only have been angered further by the court's attempts to convict him.

Simon's experience suggests that there is a good case for victim–offender reparation schemes and out-of-court mediation work. However, Simon's violent reaction to the verbal abuse was extreme, and the fact that Simon's apology was accepted does not excuse his behaviour.

Medium-term escalation of conflict

THE FUEL   Neighbours on a council estate. Few friendships.

THE SPARK   Mrs Brady buys a new door. She tells everyone how excited she is about it.

SMOULDERING   Mrs Brady is expecting the door to arrive that morning. Her neighbours are antagonised by the news. They are critical of her and her 'fucking new door', and talk about her behind her back. They are jealous and angry.

FANNING THE FLAMES   The new door arrives. Neighbours, including Mr Collins and Mrs Brent, decide secretly to telephone the council and tell them that Mrs Brady has put in a non-regulation door.

STOKING THE FIRE   The council inspector arrives, notes the door and tells Mr Collins and Mrs Brent that Mrs Brady will be reported. Mrs Brent invites the inspector in for a cup of tea. The inspector observes that the windows in Mrs Brent's house are not regulation either. They are to be reported too.

THE BLAZE   Council tenants focus their anger and resentment on the council and are united by their opposition. They are now bound together by common grievances and common needs. They refuse to pay their rent until these needs and grievances are addressed.

Notes   Where there is long-term antagonism and dissatisfaction, as here, even the smallest incident can escalate into a major conflict.

Session 23

out. If the member playing that part is not sure how to enact the suggestion, the person who made the suggestion could take over the role temporarily and try it out. In this way various ideas can be rehearsed.

All the groups share their work in this way. They can also reflect afterwards on all the other thoughts they had regarding possible interventions at other stages of the conflict.   *55 min.*

Feedback and discussion   What choices did the various characters have? Were the moments of escalation clear? What were the moments at which alternative action could have changed the situation? How did the fire analogy provide a useful focus for the study of the development of the conflict? Could participants suggest improvements to the analogy? Or develop an analogy of their own?   *15 min.*

Notes   Using the fire analogy in this way can empower people to analyse, understand and take control of their own disputes. In feedback and discussion, you might refer to the two case studies on page 165. Both case studies are based on true stories, but names and situations have been altered.

Skills   Role-play. Analysis. Group devising. Interaction.

Introduction   Exploring situations of intense conflict and examining the possibility of non-violent change. Examining alternatives to violence in bringing about change.   *10 min.*

23.2 POSTCARDS	*40 min.*
23.3 TAKING SIDES	*45 min.*
23.4 NON-VIOLENT ACTION	*45 min.*

Reflection   *10 min.*

Notes   Exercise 23.2 examines issues of social injustice and appropriate action. Exercise 23.3 examines the issues involved in taking sides in situations of conflict, and gives ideas for further exploration. Exercise 23.4 examines the variety of ways in which individuals and groups can bring about change in a non-violent manner and suggests follow-up work.

POSTCARDS

Description   A practical exercise in small groups to explore issues of social injustice and action.

Aims   To explore, through visual imagery, specific examples of social injustice. To explore possible and appropriate action.

Directions

1   Give each small group of three to five members a postcard. You can copy and cut the examples on page 168, or you can devise your own. (See the notes.) Ask each group to come up with a series of tableaux to represent the card's message. With each image they should create a sound-effect which they feel sums up its core emotion or feeling.   *15 min.*

2   The groups share their tableaux. The audience for each tableau give an account of what they think might be written on the card. Only then do the demonstrating group read out their card.   *15 min.*

3   Some groups might feel that they did not quite capture the essence of their card, or that their tableau was misinterpreted. These groups could go back and, taking on board suggestions from the audience, try to improve or change their work. (Extra time needs to be allocated for this.)

Feedback and discussion   How do the group feel about the issues raised by the cards? What action would they take if they were in similar circumstances? Are there similar things happening today? If so, what action are people taking? If participants were to sum up each card in one sentence, what would it be?   *10 min.*

Notes   It is important for the facilitator to choose cards which cover a subject matter appropriate to the group. The group could develop this work and produce their own postcards or posters.

Skills   Teamwork. Communication and clarity.

TAKING SIDES

Description   A practical exercise in small groups to explore the issue of taking sides in situations of conflict.

Aims   To explore the concept of neutrality. To explore the concept of taking sides. To explore through visual imagery the difficulties, dilemmas and challenges of intervention and involvement in situations of conflict.

Directions

1   Refer to the TAKING SIDES handout (page 169). The whole group reads the opening section (headed *Introduction*) together and discusses it. Then divide participants into three groups, each of which should take one of the three other sections (numbered 1 to 3) of the handout. (The facilitator should choose material appropriate to the group, if the TAKING SIDES handout is not suitable.)   *5 min.*

2   In small groups, participants read and discuss their section and then try to capture its essence in tableau form. Each group should create a voice-over or narration to accompany the tableau, providing a summary and a focus for the other groups.   *20 min.*

3   The groups share their work, discussing the tableaux and their subject matter.   *10 min.*

Feedback and discussion   Have members of the group ever taken sides? How and why did they do this? What current issues in their communities do they feel are relevant to this discussion?   *10 min.*

Notes   Groups could use Exercise 1.7 as a physical reminder of what it feels like to take sides. Participants could develop ideas and slogans for posters from this work. The emphasis of the exercise should be on the possibility of taking sides *without* supporting the use of violence.

Skills   Physical expression. Imagination. Communication and exploration.

POSTCARDS: THREE EXAMPLES

POSTCARD

*When I give food to the poor, they call me a saint.
When I ask why the poor have no food, they call me a
communist.*

— Dom Helder Camara, from Brazil

SOCIAL CHANGE
23.2

POSTCARD

*We are guilty of many errors and many faults, but our
worst crime is abandoning the children, neglecting the
fountain of life.*

    *Many of the things we need can wait. The children
cannot. Right now is the time their bones are being
formed, their blood is being made and their senses are
being developed. To them we cannot answer
'Tomorrow'. Their name is 'Today'.*

— Gabriela Mistral, Nobel Prize-winning poet, from Chile

SOCIAL CHANGE
23.2

POSTCARD

*First they came for the Jews and I did not speak out –
because I was not a Jew. Then they came for the
communists and I did not speak out – because I was not
a communist. Then they came for the trade unionists
and I did not speak out – because I was not a trade
unionist. Then they came for me – and there was no-
one left to speak out for me.*

— Martin Niemöller, victim of the Nazis

SOCIAL CHANGE
23.2

TAKING SIDES
Saying NO to neutrality

INTRODUCTION

YOU can take sides in a conflict situation and yet not support the use of violence. This is sometimes very difficult to do – in a situation like South Africa, for instance.

But some believe that in order to achieve reconciliation you should take on the role of a peacemaker, who avoids taking sides and tries to bring two opposing forces together. The peacemaker is fair, listens to both sides, and believes that by talking we can overcome our misunderstandings and difficulties.

SECTION 1

WHAT is wrong with the peacemaker's argument? It makes reconciliation an absolute principle that must be applied in all cases of conflict. Not all arguments are based on misunderstandings. In some conflicts one side is being oppressive and unjust, while the other side is suffering oppression and injustice. One side is right and the other is wrong. In this case, seeking consensus is clearly out of place. Why reconcile good and evil, justice and injustice? You cannot assume a neutral position between right and wrong. If we do not take sides with the oppressed, we are, however unintentionally, siding with the oppressor.

SECTION 2

'BRINGING the two sides together' hides the true nature of conflict in an unjust society. It can create a temporary truce, or a state of 'peace and quiet', but it will never create social justice. Some might say that injustice does not matter if tension and conflict are reduced, but this assumes that tension and conflict are worse evils than injustice and oppression.

Such mistaken assumptions come not simply from misunderstanding but from a lack of compassion for others, and from a lack of awareness of the root causes of conflict.

There is peace that satisfies the needs of the state. And there is peace that is just. There is a difference between peace and concord. Often superficial peace and unity compromises real and lasting peace. And sometimes one has to promote truth and justice even at the expense of conflict and dissension.

SECTION 3

IN some societies there is *structural* injustice, and here it is right to take sides with the oppressed – whatever they may be like in their personal and private lives. And the cause of the rich and the oppressor is wrong, no matter how honest and sincere and unaware they may be.

South Africa, for instance, is not a personal squabble. It is a structural conflict.

Recognition of one's enemies is important. It does not necessarily mean hating them. Nor does loving your enemy mean giving up your struggle in any way. You should try to remove all the things that make those people your enemies. In the long run, your opposition and struggle will help those people to discover their own humanity. You cannot merely attempt to convert people one by one.

Confrontation is not the same thing as hatred. Evil systems need to be destroyed, not merely replaced, for the sake of all involved.

NON-VIOLENT ACTION

Description   A group exercise exploring what non-violent action means, and drawing up steps for practical action.

Aims   To explore the area of non-violent action. To explore all the different options available. To examine a selection of non-violent options in detail. To rehearse strategies for specific action.

Directions

1   With the whole group, brainstorm the phrase 'non-violent action'. What kind of immediate responses does the term evoke? Divide into three groups to explore the following three areas: (1) The methods of protest and persuasion; (2) the methods of non-cooperation; (3) the methods of intervention. These are three distinct approaches to non-violent action, in ascending order of intensity and commitment.   *5 min.*

2   Ask the small groups to think of all the ways of responding under their specific heading. You could help, if and when it seems appropriate, by supplying examples from the list on this page.   *10 min.*

3   Each group should now prepare for a presentation to the other groups. They should choose a few examples and, by using a combination of tableaux, props, movement, voices and narration, they should dramatically give the other groups an idea of the type of action they have explored.   *10 min.*

4   From all that has been seen, a few examples should be chosen. These could be: mass petition, march, consumer boycott, sit-down, alternative transport.

The groups choose a specific action to explore in depth – a mass petition, for instance. How would they organise it? What are the first steps to take? What jobs need doing? How many people will be needed? How will they be recruited? What financial resources are needed? How will they be raised? These explorations can be shared at the end with the larger group.   *15 min.*

Feedback and discussion   What have the groups' experiences been in using this kind of action? What is the value of non-violence?   *5 min.*

Notes   A handout of quotations on non-violence would be useful as a warm-up and introduction to this section. Either prepare a sheet or encourage the group to develop its own collection.

Skills   Interaction. Communication. Planning.

NON-VIOLENT ACTION

Protest and persuasion

speeches ... statements ... letters ... petitions ... slogans ... symbols ... banners ... posters ... the media ... leaflets & pamphlets ... lobbies ... pickets ... symbolic actions ... flags ... colours ... wearing symbols ... prayer ... changing names ... vigils ... drama ... street theatre ... music & songs ... marches ... silence

Non-cooperation

boycotts ... strikes ... disobedience ... stay-at-homes ... disappearance ... withholding rent ... lock-out ... withdrawal of money ... non-payment ... embargoes ... withdrawal from institutions ... refusal to disperse ... sit-downs ... selective lawbreaking ... deliberate inefficiency

Intervention

fasting ... harassment ... obstruction ... sabotage ... raids ... occupations ... camps ... blockades ... dismantling reverse strikes ... alternative markets, transport, institutions, systems ... seeking imprisonment ... overloading the administrative systems

---

Session 24

Exercise 24.5 *Time: 130 min.*

ACTION FOR CHANGE

Introduction Examining stages in the process of bringing about social change, and working out clear strategies. *10 min.*

24.5 ACTION FOR CHANGE *130 min.*

Reflection *10 min.*

Notes Exercise 24.5 explores how the fire analogy can be used not only as a tool for analysing conflict, but as a way of understanding the process of mobilising support for a campaign, spreading the word, and achieving positive results. A practical exercise using tableaux, which gives participants the opportunity to put into practice the work of the previous three exercises.

Description Tableau work in small groups charting the progression of actions in bringing about social change.

Aims To analyse the stages involved in bringing about change. To highlight the social change we want to see. To determine the different stages for getting there.

Directions

1 Go through the stages of the fire analogy as in Exercise 22.1. Remind the group of the kind of behaviour characteristic of each stage of a conflict. In this course we have used the image of fire to help us see conflict both as potential danger and as a possible opportunity for change and creativity. We are now going to look at the blaze as something we welcome, as a fire which signifies a change we are seeking. Brainstorm with the group campaigns which have succeeded in their aims. *10 min.*

2 Ask participants, in small groups, to think about what the blaze they are looking for is. They should spend some time sharing their ideas, then choose one idea to work on. This could be something which involves the whole community, such as an end to homelessness; or it might be something which focuses on our immediate community – relieving the effects of homelessness on local young people, for instance. Whatever they choose becomes the blaze they will be working on. *20 min.*

3 Ask the participants to take each stage of the fire analogy, starting with the fuel, and assess what resources and skills they have at each stage. What must be achieved at each stage? What results are needed before they can move on? What are the key issues and aims of each stage? What action will be involved? *20 min.*

4 Ask the groups to create a series of tableaux summing up the core action of each stage. They should aim to include the practicalities of each stage, the kind of behaviour and the people who will be involved. *20 min.*

5 Watch the tableau work from each group. The following questions give some idea of what you need to be finding out from the scenes. Who is in the tableau? What are they doing?

What effect is it having? What effect will it have? What skills and resources are needed at this stage? What skills and resources are being used? What will the side-effects (positive and negative) of this be? What support do people have at this stage? What kind of difficulties will there be? Who or what will be a hindrance? How will that hindrance be countered?

45 min.

Feedback and discussion What have participants gained from this exercise? What are their practical ideas for effecting social change? How does the fire analogy help us to understand the process of change? *15 min.*

Notes Just as the fire analogy was used to facilitate analysis of conflict and its escalation, so it can be used to analyse a campaign or an action to bring about positive change. (To illustrate this, you can copy and hand out the case study on this page.) The analogy can also help campaigners to understand the process on which they are embarking, and to plan their campaign successfully. But participants should be pushed to recognise that any campaign is likely to meet opposition and difficulty.

Skills Physical expression. Interaction. Analysis. Group strategies.

Handout 24.5

CASE STUDY USING THE FIRE ANALOGY

Bringing about social change

THE FUEL Residents of Princess Road, from a variety of cultural and ethnic origins, blame each other for the noise at night in the street. Everyone has someone, or some group, to blame. High degree of antagonism in the street.

THE SPARK One family decides to initiate positive change and work towards a supportive, secure community.

SMOULDERING The family organises a meeting with two like-minded residents. Together these people plan the action they will take.

FANNING THE FLAMES They gather help and support from others. Between them they visit every house in the street, and talk to the residents about their fears, anxieties, grievances and needs. They hear from *all* the residents, not just the vocal few.

STOKING THE FIRE Many residents feel that their concerns are being heard, and want to be involved in seeing that they get addressed. They no longer feel isolated. A residents' association is set up, meeting the need for a central body which will address the grievances and fears of the residents.

THE BLAZE Residents' association in action. Regular meetings attended by large numbers of residents. Plans for setting up a local mediation scheme under way. Date for a street party set for June.

Notes The key to the success of this campaign was that the initiators listened to the needs and fears of all the residents, even those who had been involved in racist conflicts and had originally shown no evidence of wanting to change the situation co-operatively.

As soon as people began to appreciate that no-one was telling them how to behave, they gradually became open to listening to what other residents were feeling. The difficulties came to be seen as belonging to the whole community, not merely to one or another group within it, and could therefore be addressed constructively by everyone.